IN THE NOVA

SUPERHEROES AND SAVIOURS

KAJAL RANJAN

Vitasta

Published by
Renu Kaul Verma
Vitasta Publishing Pvt Ltd
2/15, Ansari Road, Daryaganj
New Delhi-110 002
info@vitastapublishing.com

ISBN 978-93-90961-79-5

First Edition 2023

MRP ₹ 399

This novel is entirely a work of fiction. Names, characters, events and incidents are entirely imaginary. Reference to real places, actual regions, institutions or community practices has been made in a fictitious manner. Any resemblance to actual persons, living or dead or actual events is purely coincidental.

Editorial Team: Shailaja Nair, Wordmeister
Layout and Cover Design by Somesh Kumar Mishra
Printed by Chaman Enterprises, New Delhi

CONTENTS

FOREWORD

Imagination is a very powerful tool. But very often, most of us brush it under the carpet, thinking that it is a vehicle for mere flights of fancy. Not so with young Kajal Ranjan. Using an imagination that literally touches the skies, she has produced a book, *In The Nova*, which talks about three different situations. Skillfully, Kajal Ranjan has inter-twined them into one humongous bundle of science fiction that can hold hands with the best of scientists and authors who work in this genre.

Kajal, who has nurtured her imagination and writing skills, has her roots in Botswana and has augmented her storytelling art from the rich tapestry of this country's cultural heritage. Her young mind has indeed produced an excellent work of science fiction that is a sure page-turner.

Flawlessly executed, this book will appeal to young and old alike and speaks volumes about the genius that this young lady is.

While congratulating Kajal for her momentous first Novel, I wish her well, and look forward to many more such achievements in the coming years.

Anup Chandra Pandey
Election Commissioner of India

FOREWORD

When I came across this series of Novellas by my young friend, it was a refreshing change, and the novelty of the concept had its own appeal. The writing skills, considering her age, are mature, and so is the imagination which has conceived brilliant storylines.

The Genre of 'Science Fiction' has always held a special fascination. Curiosity has been a continuous developmental factor for the human race; and our imagination has always played with the unknown, not necessarily to unravel a mystery or unfathom a complex phenomenon, but for the pure pleasure of getting to experience the unknown.

This is one of the most intriguing books, a compilation of compelling storytelling abilities, from a young writer who has, in her formative years, studied in the rich environs of Botswana. The art of storytelling has rich traditions in Botswana, and it gives me great pleasure to see this tradition taking root at such a tender age. The style is seamless with immaculate rhythm, deserving accolades for this first print.

The Covid-19 pandemic, severely disrupted the routine and rhythm of our social lives; it has made us feel, think, and act differently on several planes. For a while, infection had ruled the discourse, in Botswana and all over the world. Socially, the interactions have been guarded, calibrated to meet health protocols; and it all seems to unfold from some Science fiction; some even did presciently predict a pandemic afflicting the world!.

The events in this book generated a mix of emotions on several counts. It highlights a strong personal belief, that all of us are special in our own 'special' ways. The ability to change the world is inherent in all of us, especially in the 'Youth' of the day, who can redefine the future with their apt choices.

Bravery and acceptance are also on display in the poetically crafted characters in this book, reminding me of several prominent English authors who have adorned this specific genre. A rich imagination is key to our endeavours which is clearly evident here.

I wish all the best to Kajal Ranjan for her first novel and hoping to see a lot more from her in the future.

Dr. Lemogang Kwape
Minister of Foreign Affairs,
Republic of Botswana

ACKNOWLEDGEMENTS

I would like to express my deep appreciation and gratitude to my parents. They have been my number 1 supporters and never gave up on me. They let me be my creative self, let me be free with my imagination and dreams and allowed me to express myself with their full encouragement. They provided me with a caring environment filled with opportunities and endless love and inspiration. I will be forever indebted to them.

I would like to thank my grandparents for encouraging me to write. Thank you for supporting me and inspiring me to keep going, I will never forget your kindness and encouragement.

I would like also to thank all the authors that made me fall in love with fiction and books. I will always be thankful to them for introducing me to books and letting me become bewitched by the art of writing.

I have utmost respect and appreciation to all the directors and screenplay writers of science fiction films, who inspired me to be creative with my imagination and let it flow. Thank you for helping me envision my fictional theories and showing me the beauty of visualizing ideas that couldn't possibly happen… or could they?

A special thanks to the publishing and editing team at Vitasta Publishing for putting up with my edits and script format. Thank you for helping me make my goals come true

Thank you Vedaansh, for always being there for me and supporting every idea I had for this book, and listening to my ideas, even when you didn't want to. You will forever be my favorite person.

IN THE NOVA

SUPERHEROES AND SAVIOURS

THE ELEMENTS

Chapter 1

DAWN OF THE UNKNOWN

Roger: Mary, you ready?
Mary: One second, just need to get the car seat locked in, can you go to the Wilsons and get Scarlett?
Roger: I'll be back in five.
At the Wilsons' house.
Roger: Hey! Thanks for babysitting Scarlett! We really appreciate the help!
Mrs Wilson: Oh! It was nothing! Do have a safe trip!
Roger: Bye! Say Bye Scar-
Scarlett: Bye Bye!

Both make their way back home, locking the garden door for the last time.

Roger: All set?
Mary: All ready, Come on Scar, let's get you seated.

Roger goes back to the house one last time to ensure that they have packed everything. He steps out of the house, as he's about to close the door, he feels a familiar presence, the unwelcoming energy overcame him and came down flashing memories of his past, racing through his mind, looming like strong dark winds, taking over his mind like a virus. Just as fast as those memories invaded his mind, they flashed away, so did the feeling, and any recollection of this happening. He wondering why he's stopped. But doesn't give it a second thought looks back at it and closes the door. He heads back to the car. While Roger checks the car, Mary helps Scarlett into her seat.

Scarlett: Mum, what is that… on your hand? *(Points to Mary's wrist)*

Mary: Oh this? This is a bracelet your father gave me. His grandma gave it to him. She said that this bracelet had been in the family for a very long time.

Scarlett's eyes brighten.

Scarlett: It is pretty.

Mary: Well then, here you go.

Mary takes the bracelet off and ties it around Scarlett's wrist. The bracelet hangs an inch below Scarlett's hand, but she doesn't seem to mind. Her eyes appear to become brighter as she regards the dark blue colour of the bracelet. Not only that, but she feels a sense of calmness, however, she was too young to comprehend the overwhelming sense of peace.

Mary *(gently and warmly)*: Take care of it with all your heart.

Mary plants a soft kiss on Scarlett's forehead. Mary and Roger get in the car and drive to their home.

***

2 Months later

Scarlett is playing in the garden of a house with a big door and enormous blue-tinted windows. The sap green roof shone brightly under the warm sun. Mary and Roger are in a room, packing clothes. Suddenly, the wind becomes stronger, the sky turns grey, the cries of the birds grow fainter as they fly farther away. The sun disappears behind grey clouds and pets seek the shelter of their homes. Scarlett picks up the ball she was playing with as the sky darkens. When she approaches the door, she sees a black substance, taking the form of a dense, dark cloud, enter the window. The sight chills Scarlett. She runs to her parents but stops in front of the door when she sees something strange in the gap between the door and the wall. The black, cloudlike substance transforms into a man; in fact, larger than a man. The creature-if one could call it that, stood before her parents, towering the room with its broad shoulders and massive figure. Scarlett feels her throat close up as she attempts to scream out-no words come out, she is frozen.

Silence fills the house. When her vision becomes clearer, she sees that the creature is holding a long brown, viney stick, with live vines circling its height. Scarlett sees a red flame emerge, growing bigger by the second. It looked like a flame but was more than that. Before Scarlett could even comprehend what it was, it became focused and concentrated and hit Roger on his chest. Scarlett is shaken, she attempts to scream again when she sees her father fall to the ground motionless-but yet again, no words come out of her mouth.

Mary: ROGER NO! Why! Why now! Why now?!

The creature lets out a fiendish laugh while it does the same to Mary. She too falls, and lays there, motionless. Scarlett runs to the nearest closet and hides to escape the loud blaring sound of the flame. The sound stops abruptly and silence fills the house. Only the pounding sound of the clouds rubbing against each other is heard. She remains hidden till she hears a shout of anger. Scarlett's heart beats faster as the thunder and lightning fail to drown out the loud shouts, but the silence in the house was deafening.

The neighbour, on hearing the shout comes over to find Mary and Roger lying on the ground. The neighbour immediately called the police. Roger and Mary were taken to the hospital to be examined. The police searched the whole house. Scarlett was asked a few questions and then was taken to the hospital for a precautionary examination. After that, Scarlett's Aunt Claire took her to her own house in Earlsyears.

One week later, at Aunt Claire's house.

Aunt Claire: Come down Scarlett, you need to have your supper!

Scarlett comes downstairs quietly and sits beside her aunt. She barely eats anything, and spends most of her time staring into nothingness. Upon persuasion by her and, she manages to eat half her food.

Scarlett: Can I go to the park for 10 minutes?

Aunt Claire: Yes, but finish your food first. Or, promise me that you will come back and finish your food.

Scarlett: Promise.

Scarlett goes to the park in front of her aunt's house. She goes to the lake and looks down at the water. Memories of the day when her parents died flash in her mind. The police had submitted a report. Aunt Claire had said that the doctors could not find anything wrong with her parents, but their body had just stopped functioning. The police concluded that Scarlett's parents had committed suicide, and completely ignored Scarlett's eyewitness account. Aunt Claire didn't show the notice to Scarlett, but she had already read it. Scarlett knew that her parents' death was not through suicide.

Just when a tear escapes her eye, a boy, around her age, approaches her.

A boy: Hey! You have been staring into the river for half an hour. What on earth are you looking at?

Scarlett, startled, looks at the boy, and then turns back to the lake.

Small Boy: Well, my name is Chris. Are you new here?

Scarlett: Yeah. I am Scarlett.

Chris: Why did you move here?

Scarlett pauses.

Scarlett: My parents went away, so I live with my aunt now.

Chris: Uh, that sucks.

Chris pauses, not knowing what to say.

Chris: Well, do you want to go to the swings with me?

Scarlett: Ok.

Chapter 2

TWELVE YEARS LATER

Scarlett wakes up, gets ready for school, and heads downstairs.

Aunt Claire: Good-morning, dear! I made an omelette for you.

Scarlett: Thank you so much!

Scarlett gulps down the omelette as fast as she can, while making a terrible mess and on the verge of choking.

Aunt Claire: Slow down!

Scarlett: I woke up late, I need to rush. I must hand in the plan for this year to our counsellor for re-reading, then we have to give it to the principal for approval.

Aunt Claire: Good luck!

Scarlett: Thanks! Bye!

Scarlett goes to the shed to get her bike. As she cycles towards school, she spots Chris with his girlfriend. They make eye contact, but Scarlett instantly looks away and rides faster. The school Chris and Scarlett go to is called Lenz High School. The school is known for academic excellence, sports and their teamwork. Chris played soccer and basketball and Scarlett played basketball and table-tennis. Even though Lenz High School seemed perfect, socially, it was like any other high school. Division between students, social clique, and the usual drama. Everyone knew each other, and got along well, despite the class differences. Scarlett and Chia didn't get along. Chia was Chris' girlfriend. It was in middle school that Chris had started to make new friends apart from Scarlett. He was a part of several groups and clubs. Scarlett, on the other hand, was not. She was an introvert and didn't like to go up to people and start a conversation. She liked her books, sports and music. She and Chris were still good friends. Scarlett encouraged Chris to widen his circle as she saw how much it benefited him. Chris developed feelings for Chia in middle school. He didn't have the nerve to ask her, but Scarlett encouraged him to follow his heart. By the end of the term, he told Chia he liked her and she replied that she reciprocated his feelings but wanted to start as friends. In the beginning of high school, they became thick friends. As time went on, Scarlett and Chris became distant. Chris would spend most of his time with Chia and his friends from basketball practice and Scarlett would spend her time at the library, reading. Despite all this, Chris and Scarlett remained friends.

Chia never liked Scarlett. She was jealous of Scarlett's friendship with Chris. Chia spread petty rumours about Scarlett. Scarlett didn't care. If the rumour wasn't true, then she found no purpose in even thinking about it. Chia could see that the rumours never affected Scarlett. She attempted to draw a line between Chris and Scarlett, but she was never successful, and eventually gave up. However, a simple and mere mis-understanding was enough to draw a rift between the two friends. Chris was passionate about Basketball and wanted to play it in university, hoping to make a career out of it. He worked quite hard for it too. In his senior year, he had a very important game-college scouts were there to look for potential athletes. Unfortunately, he didn't get the scholarship. After that, Chris became careless, he would go out more often instead of tending to priorities, pay less attention in class-he had changed. Knowing this, Scarlett approached him about it, just to talk about it, that only worsened their relationship, it put an end to it. Ever since Chris fell off his track, rumors spread around about him, mostly about his reckless behaviour, how he became a delinquent. Most of them were far from the truth, and he didn't give them a second thought. Except this one time, it wasn't the rumor that sent him off the edge, it was the alleged person who spread it. According to Chia, Scarlett went on to tell some people about his reckless behavior and her opinions on them. Chris tried his best to keep his distance from Scarlet after learning that, but when Scarlett approached him, they both had a heavy argument, and it ended any sort of friendship they had. Ever since then, they never interacted, kept their distance from each other. Scarlett never knew the real reason why he fought with her, she never knew about the rumor.

Chapter 3

THE RETURN

Scarlett and Chris both go their separate ways after high school, Chris goes on to taking a gap year to explore and learn more about himself. Scarlett had applied for an internship program to get more on-hand experience before university. Neither of them thought they'd ever cross paths with each other, until realizing, they both were going to attend the same university. Before their first semester, the university organized camps, in order to bring in more engagement and find ways of learning, without always being inside a lecture hall.

At Orientation day, Chris and Scarlett bump into each other.

Chris: Scarlett! Wow, long time.

Scarlett almost stumbled upon her step when she saw him.

Chris: Ah watch your step-that almost got me too.

Chris helps gather the fallen books off the ground.

Scarlett: Oh, hi! - yeah - yes, it has been long.

Chris: Never stopped reading huh.

Scarlett: Ah-er yeah, always bring them around.

Scarlett paused and looked at Chris he brushed through the pages, she was reminded of how out going Chris was-it always brought a feeling of 'home.'

Chris: One day, one day I'll find out why you like them so much.

Scarlett couldn't bring words to her mouth, she could just let out a smile.

Chris: I didn't know you applied here-are you dropping off someone here?

He says, this is when she realizes, they both are going to go to camp...together.

Scarlett: I go here.

Chris: You-start university...this year?

Scarlett, unable to let out a word, nods. The atmosphere is overcome with tension. They both never talked about their argument ever since, and neither of them were as happy knowing they would be spending the next 4 years, in the same university. Just when the silence was in the edge of becoming deafeningly uncomfortable, the counsellor starts talking.

Counselor: Hi everyone, I am going to keep this short. Welcome freshmen! Hope you all have the best university experience here. In a week's time, all of you will attend camp for 4 months, to 'learn outside the lecture hall.' That is all I will say-you will be briefed on the specifics once you get to your respective destinations. As all of you are quite a huge bunch, You will be separated into groups, and will go to different destinations. You will be emailed your bus time and place. Please be prompt and punctual, and go over the checklist of recommended items you will need. If you have any questions, come to my office from 5pm to 6pm, no earlier, no later. You'll have a few days with family and friends before you take off to your 4-month camp. Good luck and enjoy.

Both Chris and Scarlett had the same thought:

"I hope I'm not with them"

One day before camp, in the evening, Scarlett walks around campus to find spot to read outside. The weather was perfect, the clouds covered the sun, a light cool breeze ran along, Silence and serenity filled the spot Scarlett found. She wanted it to be like that the whole night. It was the parents death anniversary, and nothing brings her calmness but reading her mom's favorite book outside, under the clouds, just as her mom liked to. As she makes way to the bench she found, she felt something that she hadn't felt for years – fear running through her at the speed of light. Just like on the day her parents had died. Scarlett stops walking. The wind was becoming stronger. The light coming from behind the clouds stared to further away, as darkness covered the land. She sees it – the black substance approaching her. She tries to scream but she couldn't, just like on that day 12 years ago. She tries to dodge the substance. She stumbles and falls down. When she opened her eyes, everything was back to normal. The slight warmth and light came back from behind the clouds and the wind calmed down. She hears the familiar sound approaching her. She wants to get up, but feels an overwhelming tiredness. She wants to collect her books and walk back as fast as she could back to her room to avoid any interaction with the two people she knew were approaching her. Suddenly the footsteps stop, and looks up.

Chia: Oh look who it is-Scarlett, never changed huh, always falling down. Stalking Chris again? Grow up-oh sorry, I forgot, you'll always be obsessed with him.

Scarlett knew none of those things were true, Chia wasn't making sense. Nothing was making sense to her, she felt bewildered and discombobulated. She still felt dizzy from the encounter she just had. All she wanted to do was be alone.

Chris: Don't say that to her.

Chia: Why? That's funny. I mean she is on the ground, and in the same university as you-she obviously is a stalker-her parents did something wrong, clearly.

She says with disgust and malice.

Scarlett gets up, gathers her books and looks at her bracelet. Tears fill her eyes. It is her parents' death anniversary. She longed to have her mom back, she wished she was with her parents. She doesn't give them a drop of her attention, and walks back. Chris knew it was her parents' death anniversary, he knew today was hard, but he could sense something different. They hadn't seen each other in a long time, yet he had a gut feeling something was wrong.

Chris: Chia, what are you here? We broke up a year ago and you suddenly show up?

Chia: I'm here because…my parents! Yes, my parents are alumni here, they are gonna be here any second. I just saw you, and thought of…saying hi.

Chris: Saying hi doesn't take long, you brought me here to this spot-did you do this just to play a prank on Scarlett?

Chia: What? You're taking her side now?

Chris: I never said that.

Chris sighs with frustration.

Chris: Look, its good to see you, but we're broken up for a reason, can you just let it go and leave me alone?

Chia: Ugh, why do you even care if I played a prank on Scarlett, which, by the way-I didn't. I thought you both had an argument and went your separate ways. You talked BS about her ever since then, why are you siding with her?

Chris pauses for a second, "Why am I siding with her?"

Chris: Just leave. Have a nice life.

Chia storms off leaving Chris alone, Chris debates as to if he should check up on Scarlett or not, then pauses again "Chris, get it together, why would you want to check up on her." He felt bad for Scarlett, but suppressed that emotion with the hatred he had for her.

***

Aunt Claire on the phone:

Aunt Claire: Hi! How was Orientation day, excited?
Scarlett: It was ok, yeah I guess.
Aunt Claire: I've sent a few boxes over, could you pick them up first thing tomorrow before you leave?
Scarlett: Boxes?
Aunt Claire: For camp?
Scarlett: I already have the things needed; did they send in another list to you? I didn't get an email.
Aunt Claire: Oh, erm-yes-yes they did, they sent an email… with a list of things

Scarlett sensed something was up.

Scarlett: Okay, I'll check the boxes.
Aunt Claire: Hey and one more thing, read 'guitars song' tonight, it was your mothers favorite.

Scarlett smiled, knowing her aunt would always be there for her in the toughest of times.

Aunt Claire: I miss her too, she's always here with us.

Scarlett: Thank you, you're the best.

Before going to bed, she decides to drop off her bags at the reception so that she doesn't delay.

Scarlett starts to carry the bags outside the building. Everything seems to be quiet, no one in sight, no sounds, no music from the dorms, nothing. She notices the unusual silence, but doesn't give it a second thought. When she reaches the door, she sees the same black substance inside the house. She is frozen with fear. She held onto the bag as tightly as she could, hoping that keeping a grasp on the present will prevent her from being dragged back into the past, but to no avail. She had the same flashback she had when she was on her walk to the bench. However, this time, there was something different. She could see her parents. She could see the black substance turn into a man. She saw her younger self, peeking into the room from the gap between the wall and the door. She realized that she was in the room. Normally, she would just remember just bits and pieces. But this time, it was different. She was inside the room! She wasn't inside the room when she saw what had happened to her parents, she was outside. Her strange flashback continued. She saw the fire emerge from the man's stick and hit her father, she saw the focused and concentrated flame hit her mother. Her heart beat hard, she couldn't bear the sight. She looked towards the door. Her younger self was gone. Then she saw something she hadn't seen before. She saw the strange man go towards her mother and check her hands. It looked like he was frustrated because he couldn't find what he wanted. Then, as the strange man turned, he locked eyes with Scarlett. He looked right into her eyes and Scarlett could see his green and red eyes. She thought she was invisible, but the strange man looked straight into her eyes. Before Scarlett could blink, the man turned into the black substance and raced towards her. She tried to dodge it. Just then, she returned to the present. She was standing in front of the building, still holding tightly onto the bag. She looks around her. The sun was shining brightly and everything seemed fine. She peeked through the glass door and saw her reflection in the mirror on the opposite wall.

Scarlett never really like camps. At all. That was why she never went. She preferred to stay at home, or just go to the library, when the school held camps. She was still reluctant to go to the Exponent Course, but she kept an open mind. She didn't tell Aunt Claire about what happened earlier that day because she could sense that something was off and she didn't want to risk anything. After dropping off her bags, Scarlett goes to her room and and prepares for bed. The night was quite uncomfortable, Scarlett couldn't sleep at all. She woke up at 4am, having given up on tryng to sleep. As she walks over to the bathroom, suddenly, she hears something outside the window. She draws the curtains, which squeak as the rings brush against the metal bar. Scarlett looks outside. It was dark, pitch dark. The campus building lights were off. Only the outline of the trees are visible, and the gathering clouds. Scarlett felt confused. The street lights never went off, and it was very dark. Suddenly, a streak of lightening hit the ground. The lightening didn't seem normal. It was orange in colour and emitted black particles that remained suspended in the air. Scarlett was taken aback, yet there was no sound, or any impact on anything. She froze. She could see the particles, unmoving in the air, perfectly round and black. No light passed through the particles. Scarlett tries to touch the particle. The minute she came in contact with the particles, everything that had just happened, disappeared. The clouds were gone. The setting sun could be seen in the distance. The street lights came on. Scarlett had a heavy feeling, but she couldn't figure it out. She felt she couldn't tell anyone what she was seeing for no one would believe her.

Chapter 4

LEAVING

The next day. A few hours later, Aunt claire calls.

Aunt Claire: Good Morning!
Scarlett *(still is quite tired)*: Good Morning!
Aunt Claire: Today's the big day!
Scarlett: Yeah, pretty excited.
Aunt Claire: Do you know who is in your group yet?
Scarlett: I think we'll find out once we get to the buses.
Aunt Claire: Ahh. Got the boxes packed?
Scarlett: Yes! I took a sneak peak-there are loads of clothes!
Aunt Claire: Yess! There are-you'll need them.
Scarlett: Mhmm-oh, its almost time, I should probably get going, I'll call you! Byee!

She abruptly hangs up and rushes to the bus stop.

As Scarlett runs to the bus stop she was told to go to, she gets a text from her Aunt: "Hey Scarlett-I didn't get to tell you, I wont be available to text or call, I'm going out with a group of friends to explore some place....still not sure where I'm going, but I won't be able to call you because I won't have any service. Just wanted to wish you luck-have the best time Scarlett, good luck x."

Scarlett was very confused. Her bus wasn't here, no students were in sight, and her aunt was going to go…explore? Everything was really confusion. She checked her email again to see if there was a change in plans. She groans in frustration when nothing appears. She double checks everything. She's about to give up and just head back, just when an email pops up giving the directions to another bus stop. She was confused, but didn't give it another thought and arrived at that bus stop. To her dismay, no one was there either. At this point, she thought someone was sending her on a goose chase. She waited there for 5 more minutes, just when Chris appears.

Chris: Scarlett?

Scarlett's heart drops, "we are in the same group."

Scarlett: Hi!

Chris: Yeah, uh hi-is this the bus stop? I got another email about it.

Scarlett: Apparently-this wasn't my original bus stop either.

Chris: Weird.

Scarlett: I feel like we've been sent on a-oh there it is!

Scarlett points at the bus coming towards them.

Chris: Looks like we're in the same group.

Both sigh. They both enter the bus thinking there would be more students, but the bus was empty, just as they were about to ask the driver if they were on the right bus-

A lady: Hello to the both of you! You must be wondering where everyone is-they all left-you both are late comers.

Chris and Scarlett exchange confused looks. They knew they weren't late.

Scarlett: We were told the exact times to arrive-we both were on time.

The Lady: Nonetheless, you both are late, but worry not! We will take you to your destination! Buckle in!
Chris: Are our things here too?
The Lady: All packed in!

Chris wondered to himself "Why would they have our bags-if we left them with out original buses? We didn't plan to be late..."

The bus ride starts, both Chris and Scarlet keep their dstance, but stay close-they both knew something was off, and wanted to be ready to get off the bus when they could. They stopped at a stop to grab some food. Scarlett went with Chris to get smoothies. As Scarlett was waiting for Chris to get his smootie.

She has a funny feeling, but she doesn't know why. She becomes progressively nervous. Suddenly, she stops. From the corner of her eye she saw something coming near her. The moment she turned, she realized that it was the mist again. It was rushing straight towards her. She tries to dodge it, but the coldness of the mist flows right through her. That moment (to Scarlett) lasted a minute. She could see the black particles suspended in the air. She tried to touch them again, but as she was going to, she saw a concentration of black particles move towards Chris and surround him completely. Chris was absolutely still. It was like she was looking at a wax figure or a statue. She felt an urge to warn Chris. She tried to speak, but no words or sound came out. She couldn't speak at all. She tried again. She closed her eyes and was about to scream, when she felt herself jumping back and entered reality again, literally.

Chris: Hey, are you ok?
Scarlett: Uh, yeah-Yeah, I'm ok.
Chris: You sure? Because your smoothie is about to fall.

Scarlett looks at her smoothie and realizes that she was in danger of dropping her smoothie.

Scarlett: Just caught off guard by a bee.

She could hide what happened but she couldn't hide her pale face and how frightened she was. She puts her luggage in the back of the van. Aunt Claire runs out of the house.

Chapter 5

EXPONENT

They go back to the van and settle down.

Chris: How much longer?

Driver: Ten hours.

Scarlett falls silent.

Chris: Ten hours? Apologies, but Apologies, but could we go back and get actual lunch-we didn't know the ride was this long?

Driver: We will stop at various places, you'll get food there.

Lady: The food's paid for by your university.

Chris: Great, thanks!

Chris turns to Scarlett.

Chris: You will be fine.

Chris knows that Scarlett suffered from motion sickness and that the thought of being in a car for more than two hours freaks her out.

Scarlett: I'll try.

Chris: here (as he moves his bag to where Scarlett was sitting) I've got movies and music, I'll keep you company.

Chris: We'll take movie breaks, it will be fine.

Scarlett smiles. She puts on her earphones and looks out of the window. She eventually falls asleep on Chris' shoulder. After an hour, Chris is fast asleep too. A sudden stop wakes both of them.

Lady: Dinner time!

Chris and Scarlett get out of the van.

Chris: Do you really need your bag?

Scarlett: I can't let anything happen to it.

Chris laughs.

Lady: You can go to any of these restaurants. *(Hands them a list)* Use these cards to get your dinner. Be back here by 9 pm.

Chris: Sure.

They go towards the mall.

Chris: Where do you want to eat?

Scarlett: You choose.

Chris: You sure?

Scarlett: Just choose. We'll still get to eat.

Chris: alright alright, no need to get pushy. Let's go here.

They both order food for themselves. Chris orders a full dinner while Scarlett orders a salad.

Chris: Are you gonna be full?

Scarlett: Yeah… I'm not that hungry.

It's 7:30 pm by the time they finish dinner.

Chris: We finished dinner pretty early.

Scarlett: Why don't we go to the other places, and order takeaways for us to eat later, if we can't sleep on the trip.

Chris: Off we go!

They buy food for the trip. Chris takes Scarlett to an ice-cream stand. He knew that something was up, but he also knew that ice cream always helped her. Neither of them talked much. They still hadn't talked about their argument. As much as Chris initially wanted to avoid here, he starts to enjoy her company- just like old times.

Scarlett: Thanks for the ice cream!

Chris: I had to get you something, I mean, you ate a salad for dinner.

Scarlett laughs.

Chris: It's 8:50, let's head back.

They make their way back to the van. Suddenly, lightning flashes across the sky. The same orange lightning. It seemed to light up the stars in the sky, but it made a figure, something that seemed familiar. Scarlett was caught in the moment again. She then came back to reality.

Chris: You are looking pale. Don't worry, it's just lightning.

Scarlett: Did you see that?

Chris: What?

Scarlett: In the sky? You didn't see that?

Chris: Do you mean the lightning? Yeah.

Scarlett: Yeah, the lightning... it was big...

Chris: You haven't been out much.

Scarlett: Uh huh...

Scarlett saw something familiar, but she couldn't make out what it was. They return to the van.

The driver: Ha-ha! Get in, 7 more hours to go.

On the way, Chris and Scarlett watch movies, listen to music and eat their food. They did sleep in spite of the researchers coming in and out every 15-30 minutes. They had an hour's delay because of the long lines at the petrol stations, and they reached Exponent Course only around 6 in the morning. As Scarlett steps out of the van, she is amazed by the view. The sun was rising, and the building next to them was huge. It was covered with clean polished white tiles resembling windows. It was around 7-8 stories tall, and had an enormous garden surrounding it. Scarlett and Chris walked toward the building. The pathway had beautiful bonsai plants and flowers. As they approached the door, they looked back to see if the Lady was following them because he had said that he was 'ordered' to bring their suitcases. But he was not there. Chris and Scarlett look at each other.

Chris: Wasn't he behind us?

Scarlett looks around. There was no van, and no Harrison.

Scarlett: Let's go inside, we'll ask someone inside.

They open the glass doors. The door opened into a huge room where people in suits were moving quickly from one place to another. Many people were working on computers and holograms.

Chris: What-how is it so loud in here-I didn't hear all this noise outside.

Scarlett approaches the receptionist sitting at the big circular table that had a big bold sign saying RECEPTION in golden letters.

Scarlett: Good-morning!

Receptionist: Good-morning! How can I help you?

Scarlett: We *(points at Chris and herself)* are from Exponent university, and we are here for the Exponent Course. Could you please guide us to where we are supposed to go?

Receptionist: Ah! We were waiting for you to arrive. Follow me.

Scarlett: Thank you! I also wanted to ask something else. Where are the other students? That were supposed to be in our group.

Receptionist: Apologies, but I don't have any authority to disclose any information. Come follow me, I'll direct you to our rooms.

Both Chris and Scarlett were confused, but didn't question it.

The receptionist leads them to the elevator.

Receptionist: Go to the 4th floor. Your instructor will meet you there.

The receptionist leaves them.

Chris: People here really have a bad habit of leaving their guests, don't they?

Scarlett laughs.

Scarlett: True!

Chapter 6

THE TRUTH

Chris presses the elevator button which lights up in blue. The elevator doors open. This was not your usual elevator. It had dim lights that emanated from the floor, which was made of brown tiles. It appeared incongruous, not in keeping with the aesthetics of the place. They reached the 4th floor, and when the doors opened, they saw a lady with brown hair and round glasses and wearing a blue pant suit waiting for them.

The lady: Welcome to the Exponent Course! Lovely to see you again.

Chris: Yeah, we are Chris and Scarlett.

The lady: I am Mia Adam. I will be your instructor here. Follow me, let's go on a tour.

Mia shows them around the building. She briefed them about the courses they would be taking and explains how it was different from regular learning. After their tour, they reach the 4th floor again, and she leads them into the conference room.

Mia Adam: I hope the tour was informative.

Chris: We do have one question, where are the other students?

Scarlett: Yeah-we were supposed to be in groups?

Mia Adam: Now, I am going to present to you very confidential information that is not to leave this room. You are not allowed to share this information with anyone, even if it is someone you trust a lot.

Chris and Scarlett exchange worried looks.

Mia Adam: I will not waste your time and mine by trying to be indirect, so I will be blunt. Please do not get offended. Scarlett, your parents, unfortunately passed away when you were very young. The police concluded that it was a suicide, right?

Scarlett was taken aback "How would she know about my parents? Why is she bringing it up-how is it relevant" Scarlett was about to question it, but Chris stepped in, he started to get defensive, and was on the verge of walking out. He knew this wasn't camp. They had either been kidnapped, or sent to the wrong place. Either way, he was planning to take Scarlett and leave.

Chriss: How do you know this? Who are you?

Mia Adam: Well, all cases are given to us, even if they are dismissed by the system. The cases are given to us to be archived. Your parents' case caught our eye. There were no signs of harm done to your parents. We wanted to see what could have been the case, but we couldn't figure it out. Then, we looked at what you had said about what had happened. We took that into consideration and tried to find a clue. We noticed that when-what you described… let us call it the Figure… came to your house, a very strong earthquake occurred... exactly where your house was, but there wasn't any impact. Our researchers were very surprised. They observed the seismic activity in that area, but the pattern we had predicted, failed. Then we observed very mild seismic activity where you currently lived, but they were irregular. Four months ago, there was a major earthquake near your area but again there was no impact.

Chris' eyes widen.

Mia Adam: Yes, Chris, its epicentre was your house. If I am not mistaken, your parents vanished before your eyes. Something black came by your house and then your parents vanished. We took that as a lead. We conducted our research and concluded that the figure has a connection to both of you.

Scarlett and Chris look at each other.

Mia Adam: We tried to track down the Figure. We found a place-a very remote area-where similar seismic activity was observed. We sent some of our people to investigate, but we failed to find anything. The only option left is to send you two to find this Figure. Because its effect on earth is getting bigger and bigger. The un-impactful earthquakes are somehow causing high levels of radiation. This radiation loses its energy very slowly, but when it does, it gains energy from more seismic activity. The radiation has the potential to harm millions of people.

Scarlett's eyes widen.

Scarlett: You want us to go out there and...fight the Figure? Us? University students...

Mia Adam: No, we just want you to track the Figure.

Scarlett looks scared and a little frustrated, because she feels as if those people were using them as pawns or guinea pigs. She did not want to be part of an experiment.

Scarlett: But how would we help? How on earth are we supposed to track down something that cannot be tracked by high-level experts?

Mia Adam: Do not think you are being treated as an experiment.

It's like she read her mind.

Scarlett: I do not want to be rude, but that is exactly what it feels like.

Mia Adam: Listen, you guys are our only hope. There might still be a chance to stop a mass destruction from happening.

Chris: Mass destruction?

Mia Adam: And Chris, there is still a chance we could bring back your parents.

Chris: A chance to bring back my parents? Are they still alive?

Mia Adam: We don't know. So please do not build your hopes too much.

Chris: But there is still a chance?

Mia Adam: Possibly.

There was a moment of silence. Scarlett felt she was on roller-coaster of emotions. She could not fully process what she was being told. Chris could not either. Both had to make a very big decision. Scarlett knew that her parents were dead, and there was no hope of getting them back, but she also knew that doing this could possibly save Chris' parents.

Mia Adam: Please do think about it. If you choose to join us, we will take utmost care of both of you. Your courses will continue, nevertheless. If you do not choose to join us, then, it is fine, we cannot force you to do something against your will. It would be inhuman.

Chris: Uh, we will sleep on it. Thank you, for telling us this, and thank you for believing in us.

Mia Adam: My assistant Susan is waiting outside. She will take you to your rooms. Today is your free day. You are free to explore the campus and just relax. Make yourself at home.

Chris and Scarlett approach the door.

Mia: Please, think about it.

Chris and Scarlett turn to Mia and nod.

Susan: Follow me, I will take you to your rooms.

Susan takes them to their rooms on the 6th floor. Their rooms are side by side. And Mia was right, their luggage was in their rooms. Chris and Scarlett freshen up, and settle down in their rooms. Both of them are tense and overcome with emotion. Chris has never told anyone about his parents. The police didn't believe his story, so he didn't bother to tell anyone else. That his parents could be still alive gave him hope, even though there was a big chance that they were not. He didn't know what to do. Scarlett too was overwhelmed. She thought about all the flashbacks and the lightning flashes. Maybe they were the signs of the Figure? Maybe it was trying to send her a message? Maybe it was a sign? She couldn't think straight. By the time she unpacked, it was 5:30 pm. She went to the big balcony and looked at the sunset. She needed to organize her thoughts and decide. Chris joins her.

Chapter 7

DECISIONS

Chris: Hey!

Scarlett: Hi!

Chris: Unpacked?

Scarlett: Yeah.

They both looked up at the sky. They knew that both were thinking of the same thing.

Scarlett: Your parents? Why didn't you tell anyone?

Chris: I went to the police. I told them exactly what I saw, but they wouldn't believe me. I tried telling Chia, but she thought I was pranking her. I didn't think of coming to you, but…

Scarlett: I know… we didn't really… talk much.

Chris: Yeah.

Scarlett: But you should have come to me. It isn't right, keeping something bottled up. I know things aren't really the same between us, but when something of this magnitude happens, you can't bottle it up.

Chris: I know, but it was my only option. At least the options I thought I had.

Scarlett: Just so you know, I'm always here to talk about anything.

Chris smiles.

Chris: Have you made your decision?
Scarlett: Still thinking about it. You?
Chris: Yeah. I mean I know it is risky and there is a big chance that my parents aren't alive, but just thinking about what it, the Figure, can do to other people kills me. I don't want anyone else to go through such pain.
Scarlett: Yeah… we have to at least try.
Chris: So, are you in?
Scarlett: I guess, but not because of Ms Adam. It is because, I want to.

Chris smiles at Scarlett.

Chris: We can do this.

Chris and Scarlett look into each other's eyes. They see the mixture of fear and hope in each other's eyes. The dinner bell rings.

Chris: We better go.

They dined in the big cafeteria, along with many people in suits and lab coats. The food was decent. They returned to their rooms, but they did not sleep much. The next morning, Scarlett and Chris arrive at the conference room to tell Mia their final decision.

Chris: We are in.
Mia Adam: Great! Ok, so, usually, the Exponent Course consists of a physical element and a mental element. As you are going to face the unknown, we will train you extensively in both. The training will be very hard, but you guys can do it. Have your breakfast. Then your training will start.

Chris and Scarlett start their training. Mia was right. The training was extremely hard and challenging. The fitness exercises involved rock climbing, hikes, marathon training, karate and taekwondo. They were also given life situations, which they had to solve as quickly as possible. This was very hard for them. They wanted to give up at one point but kept going. Their will to stop the Figure was strong. Over the month, they worked day and night. They had to. It wasn't easy, especially when tension between both Chris and Scarlett still existed. One would think they would surely talk it out, but both of them kept their distance. The more they trained the better they got, and so did their will to stop the Figure.

Chapter 8

LETTERS

Scarlett's letters to Aunt Claire.

Dear Aunt Claire,

Hi! How are you? How is everything going? I wish you were here. The first week here was so bizarre. There are so many new things to learn. There are computers in every room, but these computers are not normal computers, they are of next level! The screens are very thin, and the computers vary in sizes! There are computers that are actually holograms, but still work like a computer, well more like a touch-screen computer. Despite how high-tech Exponent Course is, they have a huge library! It has really long shelves of books, ranging from fiction to non-fiction. The course is really hard. I mean, I do enjoy it, but it does challenge us a lot. We have to do so many fitness exercises and mental challenges. Like puzzles. It was much harder than I thought, but it is fun. At least, I'm learning new things that will help me. I actually thought we would learn higher level subjects but I don't think they do that here. Write back to me. I miss you!

—Scarlett

****

Dear Scarlett,
I am so happy you are enjoying yourself, I told you that you would have fun. Everything As time has passed, things are is great. The bed is not as soft as my own, but it is comfortable. I've learnt so much about other cultures-and it's only been a month! The people I'm with are really amazing too-but there is drama-loads of it, when I come back-I am definitely spilling the tea. I miss you too!

—Claire

****

Dear Aunt Claire,
As time has passed, things are lot easier as I have got the hang of the exercises. Chris and I had to go rock-climbing. It was a lot of fun but we had to climb in a set amount of time. You know, the library is open 24/7, which means I can access it anytime. The library has become my comfort zone. It is really quiet in there and I was wrong. We do have to do higher level subjects. I am so excited about that. Especially physics. I know that it would be hard, but I am in! I'm so happy you are having a great time! And Yes! I'm definitely looking forward to the tea. You can do it.

—Scarlett

Chapter 9

THE SEARCH BEGINS

Two months later.

Gary: Come on! Come on! Come on! And… time!

Scarlett is trying to catch her breath. She puts her hands on her knees to balance herself.

Gary: You set your record!

Scarlett (still trying to catch her breath): Great!

Gary: Go get water.

Scarlett stands up and gives a high-five to Chris.

Chris: Nice! New record!

Chris gives the water bottle to Scarlett.

Scarlett: Still haven't caught up with you.

Chris: You'll get there.

The next month and a half was much more easier for the both of them, and surprisingly enough, they started to become genuine friends again, and act as if nothing ever happened, as if the argument never existed.

Mia Adam: Well, this has been a rough month and a half for you two, haven't they?

Chris: They have.

Mia Adam: You've done well and progressed well especially in the physical element. I called you here to tell you that you will be going tomorrow.

Chris *(hoping it wasn't to track down the Figure)*: To another level of training?
Mia Adam: Chris, you know where. You are going to track down the Figure tomorrow.
Scarlett: Why did you tell us this now? We would have prepared more if we had known beforehand.
Mia Adam: Actually, you weren't supposed to go until next month, but the researchers on this project have detected seismic activity at our site, and the pattern of activity is more frequent now, which indicates that whatever the Figure is planning to do, he is going to do soon.
Scarlett: Ok, so, we are going tomorrow. Are our necessary equipment packed? I mean, we would need something to defend ourselves-we need to pack all the things that we've been using-that's going to take time-how are we going to prepare so soon.

Scarlett started to worry even more. Despite the hard work she's done over the month, she doesn't feel ready.

Mia Adam: Don't worry, your backpacks are full of all the necessary equipment, food and a lot of water.
Chris: How long will we be out there?
Mia Adam: We don't know.
Chris: Then, what if our food and water run out?
Mia Adam: The site has a lot of natural foods that you can eat and you will find potable water on the way. The people we sent have confirmed this.

Aside the fact that Chris looked the organization up for reliability-the organization him and Scarlett are working with, he still didn't have full trust in them. Potable water? If the people they've sent know about it-why weren't they the ones to go on the mission? They surely should have been first priority. Chris kept quiet about this, he didn't want to create any sort of problem or worry Scarlett. The only thing that kept him from asking and question the organization's motives, was his parents, and the slight chance that he could save them-from whatever malicious creature took them.

Mia takes out some small things that resembled two computer chips and small speakers. She offers them to Chris and Scarlett.

Mia Adam: These are trackers and an earpiece. This will help us see where you are at all times. We can send signals through these chips to communicate with you and there are certain spots where we can contact you through the earpieces. It will be like checkpoints, so that we know that you are safe and on track. We will be able to tell you if you are entering a danger zone, or a zone where you wouldn't find the Figure at all.

Scarlett: Is there a physical map that we can have so that we can navigate the path ourselves?

Mia Adam: Well yes, we do, but not of the whole area. We only have the parts our people have covered. We will give those maps to you tomorrow. You can relax today. Gather your thoughts and get ready for the challenge.

Chris: So, we don't have classes today?

Mia Adam: No. Take the time to reflect and build your confidence. We will wake you up very early in the morning, so get a good night's sleep. Dismissed.

Chris and Scarlett make their way back to their rooms. They clean their room. They both catch a good 3-hour nap. Scarlett goes out for a walk and spots Chris.

Scarlett: Hey!

Chris: Hey!

Scarlett: You ready?

Chris: I don't think I would know if I was ready.

Scarlett: Yeah, we are facing the unknown.

Chris: And the unknown is what scares mankind the most.

Scarlett: Well, we can't stay scared forever.

Chris: Yup. (sighs) We can do this.

Chris holds Scarlett's hand. Scarlett is quite shocked-she'd never expect Chris to do that, but she yearns for the warmth and home feeling he radiates.

Scarlett: We can do this.

The next day Scarlett was already in the lobby at 4 am. Chris joins her at 4:15.

Chris: Today is the day.

Scarlett: Yup.

Chris: Good luck out there.

Scarlett: You too.

Mia takes them to the control centre. She gives them their equipment, briefs them on the necessary things, gives them a map, and then takes them underground to a dark tunnel. She tells them that the tunnel will lead them to the site, and from there, they will need to track the Figure on their own using the research done by others.

Mia Adam: That is all for now. You can use the flashlight in the tunnel because it is quite dark, but there is only one way this tunnel goes so you can't lose your way. Good luck!

Chris and Scarlett step into the tunnel. It had a cement/rock smell. It was as if no one had walked through this tunnel for a long time.

Scarlett: Maybe we shouldn't waste the flashlight's battery.

(Scarlett's voice echoed in the tunnel)

Chris: You're right but how are we going to know that both of us are still here? I mean, we can't talk forever.
Scarlett: Maybe attach our bags with some kind of rope.
Chris: Ok.

They try to link themselves with a rope but it is difficult to do so in the dark.

Chris: This is complicated. Maybe we just hold hands?
Scarlett: Sure.

They evolve a strategy. They would walk for 15 minutes, jog for 10 minutes, and then interchange this strategy so that they would not get dehydrated or tire too quickly. Their strategy works. They use their glowing watches to keep track of time and successfully reach the end of the tunnel. They try to adjust to the daylight. It had taken them about 45 minutes to cross the tunnel. They step into a place that looks as if no human had ever walked there. It was like they had entered a time way before humans had evolved. The place had a lot of greenery, high levels of moisture and many trees and flowers.

Scarlett: Woah, this is amazing!
Chris: Uh huh, truly. I don't think humans are the major species on this land.
Scarlett: Even though that is amazing, it also means that there are many predators here. We need to be careful from now on.
Chris: You are right. We need a plan. How would we fight off an animal if attacked?
Scarlett: I thought about that. I know this is shallow, but I packed extra bottles with meat inside. We could distract them using the meat.
Chris: Great! Awesome, how did you get it past security? (he says with a sheepish look)

Scarlett: Just snuck it in when they weren't looking.
Chris: Wow-look at that! The goody two shoes is evolving! (Chris says in the most sarcastic tone he could let out)
Scarlett (as she rolls her eyes)**:** Oh please!

Chapter 10

THE FIRST ENCOUNTER

Scarlett hands Chris two bottles and they continue on a path as instructed by Mia and her team. They walk on for a long time. They stop suddenly. There was something in the bushes. Their chips warn them with a turn back signal.

Chris: The chip signal says we must turn back.

Scarlett: But we have made it this far, why turn back now?

Chris: I don't know. Maybe we are in a danger zone.

Scarlett: Chris, we came here to track down the Figure. We can't do that if we turn back.

Chris: But it's an order.

Scarlett: I know, ahhh ok, let's turn back.

They turn around and realize that the sound was that of an animal. It wasn't any ordinary animal, it was like a hybrid of a lion and a bear. Scarlett and Chris turn pale.

Chris: Bear!

Scarlett: Lion!

Chris: What do we do?

Scarlett: Run!

Chris: We can't do that. The bear might run after us.

Scarlett: But a lion's first instinct is to catch its prey!

Both Chris and Scarlett in unison: The meat!

They both take some meat out and throw it behind them. Surprisingly, the lion-bear took the bait and ran after it. Scarlett and Chris seize the opportunity and run in another direction, and hide. Scarlett sprays deodorant on both of them.

Chris: What the heck?

Scarlett: We smell like humans. We don't need that scent, or the lion-bear...whatever it is, could find us.

Chris: Oh okay.

They remain still for about 4-5 minutes. Then Chris leaves their hiding spot to check if the predator was still there. It wasn't.

Chris: You can come out. It's gone.

Scarlett: Damn, that was intense.

Chris: It was.

Scarlett looks at her map.

Scarlett: Well, the detour we took was in the right direction. We have to follow this path for about 10 minutes to get to Checkpoint 1.

Chris: Let's go.

Chris: You thirsty?

Scarlett: Not really. You?

Chris: Nope.

They reach Checkpoint 1. Immediately their earpiece contacts the control centre and they hear Mia's voice.

Mia Adam *(through the earpiece)*: Can you guys hear me?

Both Chris and Scarlett: Yes, we can hear you.

Mia Adam: Good that you are safe. Why didn't you follow the order?

Scarlett: We did, but we were attacked by an animal because of it.

Mia Adam: That wouldn't have happened if you had listened to the order sooner. You have to come back.

Chris: What?

Mia Adam: It is too dangerous.

Chris: Then why did we train for two months?

Mia Adam: It is an order. It is not safe. We cannot guarantee safety.

Chris: We don't need your guarantee. We came here, not because of you, but because we want to get rid of the Figure. We have come all this way, we cannot turn back.

Mia Adam: We are losing connection, come back. That is an order.

Scarlett heads in the opposite direction.

Chris: Wait!

Scarlett: What?

Chris: We can't go back.

Scarlett: It was an order. We have to.

Chris: Scarlett, we came all this way. We can't stop now.

Scarlett: I know, I understand. I also want to keep going, but they know where we are at all times.

Chris Pauses for a moment, then takes his chip and ear piece and throws them into a nearby stream. Scarlett's eyes widen. Chris can see she is worried.

Chris: Scarlett, there is a chance my parents are alive. I want to at least try to save them. If I don't, I'll blame myself every day for not grabbing that opportunity. I also care about you, so, you should go back to the control centre, you'll be safer there.

Scarlett looks at Chris. She couldn't bring her parents back, but if she didn't help Chris find his, she wouldn't be able to forgive herself. Scarlett takes her chip and earpiece and throws them into the stream too.

Scarlett: I'm coming with you. I'm not going to leave you.

Chris smiles.

Scarlett: Let's go.

As they are walking.

Chris: Hey, where did you get that bracelet?

Scarlett: From my mom. Why?

Chris shows her his necklace. It had the same teal gem.

Scarlett: Whoa, where did you get that?

Chris: From my dad.

Scarlett: Does it have a waterfall carved on the other side?

Scarlett shows him the carving of a waterfall on the other side of the gem. Chris flips his necklace and sees a volcano.

Chris: It's a volcano.

Scarlett: Whoa, that is a weird coincidence.

Chris: Yup.

It is now dusk. Scarlett and Chris try to find a place where they can settle down and light a fire. They find a small empty space. They collect logs and start a fire. They lay out a mat and food and start eating.

Chapter 11

THE PAST

Chris: Hey, can I ask you a question?
Scarlett: Shoot!
Chris: What happened to us?
Scarlett: Friendship?
Chris: Yeah.
Scarlett: Well, that-
Chris and Scarlett in unison: Argument.
Chris: Yeah.

Silence fell upon them. None of them knew what to say. Just as Scarlett tried to change the subject, Chris broke the silence.

Chris: Why did you spread that rumor about me? Like, I knew people were talking about me, and how I changed, but why did you say that? I wouldn't have ever expected you to say something like that. Why couldn't have you just come to me and told me?
Scarlett: Rumor? What rumor?
Chris: That I was being reckless, drinking and smoking-
Scarlett: What? I never said that?
Chris: But Chia-

And that's when he realized, he never gave Scarlett the chance to explain herself, Chia was lying.

Scarlett: Since day one, Chia has been trying to ruin our friendship-I guess she succeeded.
Chris: Why didn't I see it coming? How did I believe that back then?
Scarlett: hey-it's okay, you were in a relationship and in love! You wouldn't have thought of anything otherwise. Plus, we weren't that close anyway in senior year.
Chris: But we could have been. I miss it, us, our friendship.
Scarlett: Same, I've missed it too.
Chris: Chia and I have broken up.
Scarlett: When?
Chris: That doesn't matter. What happened? End of senior year, I finally got my brain to start working and see past her "act." She was cool back in middle school, but something changed in high school.
Scarlett: Mhmm. I do miss us, a lot.

Chris leans close to Scarlett and kisses her on the cheek.

Chris: I uh…
Scarlett: It's ok.

The next day, they continue to follow the path indicated on the map, but then they realize that they are back where they had started.

Scarlett: Chris!
Chris: Yeah?
Scarlett: We are back where we started.
Chris: No, we are…
Scarlett: This is where we threw our chips.
Chris: Damn it! But we followed the map!
Scarlett: We did, but the map is wrong.
Chris: What do we do now? Argh!

Scarlett: Don't be frustrated.
Chris: How can I not be? We came all this way and-
Scarlett: Calm Down! Dude! We'll get there. We need to get our heads straight.
Chris: You're right.
Scarlett: Ok, so, let us think about it like this. The Figure has something to do with us or our parents. He must want something that both our parents have.
Chris: But what could that be?
Scarlett: Our jewellery!
Chris: What?
Scarlett: My bracelet and your necklace! Our parents had them before.
Chris: Yeah, yeah… so we wait until he comes to get us?
Scarlett: No, you have a volcano on yours, right? We passed a huge volcano.
Chris: And we also passed a waterfall.
Scarlett: Maybe that is our clue.
Chris: Should we start with the volcano?
Scarlett: It's our first lead. Let's go!

They go towards the volcano.

Chris: Hey, wait a second. How do we know that the volcano won't erupt any second?
Scarlett: Well, the research Exponent did say that the volcano had been inactive for a very long time.
Chris: How do we know that they are right?
Scarlett: Hmm...Even though their map was completely wrong, the researchers at Exponent concluded that the volcano is inactive as it hadn't erupted in a very long time.
Chris: Well, let's hope they are right.

Chapter 12

THE STORM

After a few hours, they had their lunch and kept going.

Chris: We are close to the volcano.

Scarlett: Yeah…

Looks suspiciously toward the volcano.

Chris: What's up?

Scarlett: It's weird. There is a big, plane, bright green area surrounding the volcano.

Chris: Yeah, so?

Scarlett: That isn't natural.

Chris: Well, I mean, a lion-bear isn't natural either.

Scarlett: I guess, but how would we get past it without being noticed? I mean, it would be very noticeable if two people walked there.

Chris: We'll just have to see. Maybe there is another way out.

They reach the part where the green patch starts. They start walking toward the volcano very cautiously, hoping that they would not be spotted. Suddenly they felt the ground tremble.

Scarlett: What the heck?!

Chris: Scarlett…RUN!!!

They run as fast as they could in the opposite direction. Trees begin to emerge from the ground and fill the large patch. The rate at which the trees emerge is very fast. They manage to escape and reach a higher level.

Scarlett: Oh my gosh! What was that?

Chris: Oh no!

A huge tornado is heading their way.

Scarlett: We need to find cover.

Chris: I can't hear you!

Scarlett catches hold of Chris' hand and they both run to find cover behind a tree. Fortunately, the tornado dies down, but the wind is still blowing hard.

Chris: Do you think that the tornado will build up again?

Scarlett: There is a big chance that it might, maybe we should-

Chris: Look out!

Chris tightly grips Scarlett's hand and they both fall into the bushes. They are very uncomfortable. Scarlett doesn't have any space to move.

Scarlett: What-

Chris: Shhh! *(whispers)* Look!

Chris points at the lion-bear that is coming closer to them. The lion-bear comes so close that if Scarlett reaches out, she would be able to touch its fur. Suddenly, a sword cuts through the lion-bear and a loud shriek is heard. Chris and Scarlett could barely grasp what had happened. They both try to get out of the bushes. They make out a human silhouette. They finally break through the bushes and see Mia Adam.

Both Chris and Scarlett: Ms Adam?

Mia Adam: Hi! Nice to see you again… alive!

Chris, Scarlett and Mia find a spot to sit down.

Chris: How did you find us?

Mia Adam: I found your water bottles.

Takes out a green bottle and a red bottle.

Mia Adam: You guys really saved up for water, huh?

Scarlett remembers that there was meat in those bottles, not water. She becomes suspicious of how Mia found them.

Mia Adam: Now, will you both please tell me why you threw your chips and earpieces into the stream?

Scarlett thinks to herself: "How does Ms Adam know that we threw our chips and earpieces?" She grows even more suspicious.

Chris: Well, we both trained intensely for two months. We didn't want to throw all that away. And we had just started. You couldn't have thought that we would give up so easily.

Mia Adam: I guess. But, do not disobey an order again.

Scarlett: But why are you here?

Mia Adam: Well, we did not know where you were, and we did not want to lose you guys so easily.

Chris: Couldn't you have just sent out a team?

Mia Adam: I couldn't. Otherwise they would have found out my secret.

Chris: Secret?

Mia Adam: I know where the Figure is.

Scarlett and Chris exchange confused looks.

Mia Adam: Well, a few years ago, the Figure took my husband, and that is what motivated me to find it. I did a lot of research, and I think I have a lead.

Chris: Well, uh, Scarlett and I actually-

Scarlett nudges Chris and looks at him. He realises that Scarlett didn't want him to tell Mia about their lead.

Chris: Found a much unexpected creature, do you know its name? I figured that you would know the creature's name through the research you did.

Mia Adam: Well, if you describe the creature, I'll have a look at my research and check it out.

Chris is a little surprised at Mia's choice of words. She had never used 'check it out' before. Suddenly, she looks at her watch, which doesn't really look like a watch.

Mia Adam: Look at the time! We should bring in wood for the fire. I'll get it.

Chris and Scarlett exchange confused glances as the way Mia Adam was acting was way out of her normal character. Mia walks into the deep forest.

Chapter 13

DECEPTION

Mia Adam reaches a house. She enters the house and her appearance changes. Two other people appear in the room from the dark.

Person 1: Hey, Ms Adam!

Person 2 starts to laugh, then immediately stops when he sees the look on the face of the fake Mia Adam.

Person 2: Vicky, stop it. Jeanie is superior to us.

Vicky: Oh Brock, come on, a little fun never hurts.

Jeanie: Shut up, both of you.

Person 1 is Vicky, Person 2 is Brock and the fake Mia Adam is Jeanie.

Jeanie: The plan is in play.

Vicky: So, do we get to beat up Scarlett and Chris now?

Jeanie: No. Don't you remember the plan?

Vicky is silent.

Jeanie: Master has given us this task, and we have to carry it out successfully, or you know what will happen. Now, I am not going to repeat this again, so listen carefully, and engrave this into your dumb brains!

Both Brock and Vicky take a step back, slowly.

Jeanie: I have successfully fooled Chris and Scarlett into thinking I am Mia Adam. Once they are asleep, we will separate them and take what we want. At midnight, both of you will turn into Chris and Scarlett to deceive them. I will clone myself so that nothing seems too suspicious. Brock, as Chris will come with me and Scarlett to Cabin 1, and Vicky, as Scarlett you will go with my clone and Chris to Cabin 2. And don't blow your disguise, or you know what will happen.

Brock: Yes, we disintegrate, and then come back to life with the same memories but with a different personality.

Jeanie: Once we have a hold on them, we can easily get what we want, and give it to the Master.

Vicky: Why do I get Cabin 2? It's shabby.

Jeanie glares at Vicky.

Jeanie: Do as I say. I have been here for too long. Brock, do you have the wood?

Brock: Yes.

Jeanie, Vicky and Brock, all work for the Figure. Jeanie is going to fool Chris and Scarlett and get what the Master wants. Jeanie turns into Mia Adam again and goes back to Chris and Scarlett.

Jeanie: So sorry I took so long. It was hard to find the wood.

Chris: Oh, it's ok!

They set the fire going.

Chris: We still have food left. I'll get it out.

Jeanie: Oh, don't worry, I brought some.

Scarlett: Ms Adam, it's ok! We should store that for later.

Jeanie: But this food might rot sooner.

Scarlett: Oh ok. Thank you so much!

Chris and Scarlett heat up the food. They have absolutely no idea about what is going on. They genuinely believe that it is in fact Mia with them. They don't know what is coming to them. They have their food.

Scarlett: So, what is the plan?

Scarlett starts feeling dizzy.

Scarlett: Sorry, I don't know why I'm feeling sleepy.

Scarlett and Chris drop to the ground. They are sound asleep.

Jeanie: Now, now… The plan has just begun! *(Laughs loudly)*

Chapter 14

CHRIS' PATH

Jeanie clones herself into another Mia Adam. Brock changes into Chris and Vicky changes into Scarlett. Jeanie, Brock (as Chris) take Scarlett to a cabin deep in the forest. Vicky and Jeanie's clone take Chris to another cabin, also deep in the forest, but farther away from Cabin 1. Chris wakes up in the cabin. He is very confused.

Chris: Scarlett? Ms Adam?

Vicky: Quit yelling!

Chris: Oh Scarlett! I thought something happened to you. Where are we? Where is Ms Adam?

Jeanie's clone: We found a cabin in the forest. We tried to wake you up, but you didn't budge.

Chris: So, you carried me all the way here?

Jeanie's clone: We didn't have a choice.

Vicky: You were really heavy, like really heavy! And you sleep talk! It was very funny! Hahaha!

Chris is surprised. He never expected Scarlett to be mean. Jeanie's clone glares at Vicky because she was in danger of blowing the cover.

Jeanie: Now, now it happens. From here, we need to exit this forest and then head north.

Chris: How do you know that?

Jeanie's clone: My research says that the Figure is stationed somewhere there. The map will help us get there.

Chris: Research? You keep mentioning research, but never actually show us anything, and the map is completely wrong. When I and Scarlett followed it, we went round in a circle, right Scarlett?

Vicky: Oh yeah, Ms Adam, we tracked down Mast… the Figure (she says while emphasizing 'the figure' and almost bursts into laughter on the sound of the name). And we came to another route.

Jeanie's clone glares at Vicky.

Jeanie's clone: Ok, we will follow your route, Chris.

Chapter 15

SCARLETT'S PATH

Scarlett wakes up in another cabin. She is very confused. She rubs her eyes, trying to make out where she is. She calls out for Chris.

Scarlett: Chris? Hello?

Brock: Gosh, finally, you're up.

Scarlett is relieved to see Chris. She jumps out of her bed and runs to 'Chris' to give him a hug.

Scarlett: Where are we?

Brock (as Chris) gestures that he does not like the hug and he wants to get out. Scarlett immediately knows that something is wrong. She knows that Chris wouldn't act like this.

Brock: We are still in the forest. We found this cabin, so we came here.

Scarlett: How do I not remember coming here?

Brock: You were sleeping. Ms Adam and I tried to wake you up, but you didn't budge, so we had to carry you here.

Scarlett was surprised because she is usually a light sleeper and she would have woken up at least when they carried her. She didn't remember sleeping last night and is surprised that Chris said "Ms Adam and I." He usually gets that grammar wrong, he would normally say "Me and Ms Adam."

Scarlett: Oh!

Jeanie: Ah, Scarlett! You are up. I am assuming you had a good sleep.
Brock: Considering she had 14 hours of sleep! What is the plan?
Jeanie: We are going to stay here today as the weather doesn't look too good. We will find the Figure tomorrow.
Scarlett: Why would we waste a perfectly good day? I mean, even though the weather isn't the best, we cannot waste any more time. Chris and I went through a crazy storm, I don't think a bit of bad weather will affect us much, right Chris?
Brock: Scarlett, we need to obey Ms Adam. We shouldn't have crush… thrown our chips and earpieces away.

Scarlett knew that 'Chris' was about to say crushed. She instantly put two and two together and realized that Ms Adam and Chris aren't actually who they said they were. Through the day, she spends her time in the room she had slept in. She used her time to gather her thoughts and come up with an escape plan. She plans to slip out when both of them are asleep. She doesn't know where she'll go, but her first step was to get out of that place. When night falls, they all have dinner and go to sleep. When Scarlett is positive that everyone is asleep, she tries to slip out through the window. But halfway out, she froze.

Brock: Scarlett, Scarlett, Scarlett! I never thought you were the wisest person.
Scarlett: Who are you? (asks sternly)
Brock: Oh Scarlett, wouldn't you like to know!
Scarlett: You aren't Chris, and Ms Adam is not who she says she is. I am guessing you work for the Figure.
Brock: Maybe I was wrong. You are a little smart, but still not smart enough.

Brock goes close to Scarlett.

Scarlett: Get away from me!

Brock: You have to be smarter! The Figure is not bad, he is fighting for the good. You have been manipulated into thinking that the Figure is bad and evil, but he is not.

Scarlett: It killed my parents!

Brock: For a REASON! He was trying to save you. Your parents hated you. And… you know what, I have had enough of this. Give me what I want.

Scarlett: What do you…

In a rage, Brock jumps on Scarlett. He fights with her. She fights back but was no match for him. Scarlett was on the verge of collapsing, but she gathered all her might and punched Brock as hard as she could. To her surprise, Brock instantly disintegrated into dust. Scarlett could not believe her eyes. Jeanie walks in.

Jeanie: What is going on? Why are you shouting?

Scarlett: Chris… wait not Chris…

Scarlett started to panic.

Scarlett: Chris exploded into dust.

Ms Jeanie: What are you saying?

Brock's second version walks into the room, still disguised as Chris. This is because he blew his disguise. And when he blew his disguise, he disintegrated and became a new version of himself, with same memories, but different personality.

Brock: What is going on? Why so much noise in the middle of the night?

Jeanie: Scarlett was sleepwalking. Scarlett, you need to go to bed right now.

Scarlett: Oh no, you don't tell me what to do. You are not Ms Adam and you are not Chris. WHO THE HECK ARE YOU?

Brock: Jeanie, she caught us out.

Jeanie: Well then, now we can get what we want.

Scarlett charges for the open window.

Brock: Oh Scarlett! You innocent little wimp!

Brock grabs a vase and throws it at Scarlett. Scarlett ducks and dodges the vase, which shatters into a hundred pieces. Brock and Jeanie duck for cover. Scarlett takes this opportunity to escape from the room, Jeanie and Brock in hot pursuit. Jeanie picks up a saucepan and hits Scarlett on the face. Before Scarlett can recover, Brock punches her. Scarlett collapses on the ground.

Jeanie: Oh no! Did we kill her?!

Brock: Weren't we supposed to do that?

Jeanie: No! She has to be merely unconscious. The Master wants her alive.

Brock: Ok, ok, calm down.

Jeanie: CALM DOWN!? HOW AM I SUPPOSED TO CALM DOWN WHEN WE have KILLED HER?

Brock Let's not jump to conclusions. Let me check her pulse.

Brock reaches down to feel Scarlett's pulse. She grabs grabbed the pepper spray from her pocket and sprays it into Brock's eyes.

Brock: ARGHHHHHHHH!!! You son of a…

Brock lets out a cry of pain and collapses on the floor. Scarlett and Jeanie start to fight. She wasn't really sure if she was dealing with a human being or not, but she tried her best to render Jeanie unconscious. And she did it. She noticed a paper in Jeanie's hands. She took the paper (thinking it may be useful in some way), grabbed her things and ran out of the cabin.

Chapter 16

THE UNFORTUNATE JUNCTION

Chris still thinks he is with Scarlett and Ms Adam. He leads Vicky and Jeanie along the route that Scarlett and he had initially decided on. But they walked in a circle for over three hours. They were back at the cabin.

Vicky: Gosh! We just wasted three whole hours!

Chris: I thought we were…

Vicky: No one cares what you think!

Jeanie's clone: Maybe now, it's best if you listen to me.

Chris was now convinced something was up. Scarlett was acting out of character, and as much as he didn't trust Ms Adams, he knew this isn't how she acts.

Jeanie's clone: We will stay here at the cabin for the night, and then follow 'my' plan tomorrow.

Night falls and they go to sleep. Chris closes his eyes and tries to sleep, but he can't. He suddenly hears a noise. He opens his eyes to see Vicky holding a saucepan right above his head.

Chris: Scarlett! What the heck?

He pushes Vicky and she disintegrates. Chris is shocked by seeing Vicky, as Scarlett, turn into dust.

Jeanie: What is going on? Why are you making so much noise?

Chris: Ms Adam, something terrible has happened. Scarlett was going to…

The other version of Vicky emerges from the darkness, still disguised as Scarlett.

Vicky: What is going on?

Chris: You were about to hit me!

Vicky: Why would I hit you?

Jeanie: You know what, we have very little time to rest. I am going back to bed, please don't argue loudly.

Chris: You were going to hit me.

Vicky: I would never! Chris, we have been friends since we were kids, and recently, I have developed feelings for you!

Chris: You acted so maliciously towards me today, and now this. Scarlett, I can't do..what ever this is. Let's talk tomorrow.

Vicky: I thought we had something special!

Vicky goes to Chris and hugs him. He becomes even more uncomfortable and pulls away.

Chris: Let's talk tomorrow.

Vicky: Okay.

Chris waits for about an hour and then tries to slip out. But he gets caught by Jeanie.

Jeanie: You are so silly and idiotic. Do you really think that you could escape?

Chris: Who are you?

Jeanie: At least, you are wiser than Scarlett.

Chris: What did you do to her?

Jeanie: What she deserves! Join us… the Figure always means good.

Chris: He killed Scarlett's parents.

Jeanie: But not yours.

Chris is speechless. His anxiety ebbs when Jeanie mentions that his parents are alive.

Jeanie: Yes Chris, your parents are alive and well. If you come with us, then you will get to meet your parents.

Chris really wants to meet his parents. But Scarlett is still out there. If he doesn't go with them, he might never be able to meet his parents.

Jeanie: Come with me, you know you want to.

Chris shakes his head and thinks to himself: "What are you thinking? She may be lying? Are you really thinking of going with someone who wants to kill you?"

Chris: No!

Jeanie: That was your biggest mistake. And your last!

She charges at him and grabs him by the throat. He struggles to break free. Vicky then comes behind Jeanie and hits her with a bat. Jeanie disintegrates. Vicky has had enough of Jeanie. She knew that she still had to carry out the task, which she decided to do without Jeanie.

Chris: Oh My Gosh! Di…did you see that?

Vicky: Yeah. Are you okay?

She hugs Chris. Chris still is quite skeptical, but is comfortable with her.

Chris: Yeah, thanks to you, but I still don't understand.

Vicky: It was all part of my plan. I could also smell something fishy about Ms Adam. I have observed her all day. I knew something was up, so I used the technology from Exponent to make another version of me, as a hologram, and because the technology is very advanced, it looked as if I actually disintegrated. But it was just the hologram.

Chris: But… I felt you.

Vicky: It's the new feature in the software. But enough of that.

We need to get out of here.

Chris: You're right. But where do we go?

Vicky: Anywhere but here. I guess we could just walk and see where it leads us.

Chris: Wow, I've never seen you being so random.

Vicky: It's a new thing I'm trying.

Chris: I need to go to the bathroom.

Chris goes to the bathroom and sees a piece of paper lying in the basin. He picks it up. The paper is very soft. It was some sort of map. His gut told him to keep it.

Chris: Let's go.

Chris and Vicky walked as far as they could from the cabin. It was very dark, so they didn't really know where they were going. They walked for hours. The light started to slowly fill the sky.

Vicky: Chris, I am tired.

Chris: We could wait here for a while.

Vicky: Great idea...

The bushes moved; someone was coming their way.

Chris: Scarlett, stand behind me.

Vicky did as she was told. Scarlett emerged from the bushes. Chris was very confused and shocked.

Chris: Scarlett?

Scarlett: Chris?

Chris stepped aside and rubbed his eyes. He was actually looking at two Scarletts.

Chris: Scarlett?

Vicky was in a panic.

Vicky: Who is she?

Scarlett: Who is she?

Chris: Oh my, this is a disaster!

Vicky holds Chris' hand.

Vicky: Chris, who is she?

Chris: I have no idea.

Scarlett: Chris! She is not me!

Vicky: What do you mean? I am Scarlett.

Scarlett: No, I am! Chris, you cannot possibly think that she *(points at Vicky)* is Scarlett!

Chris is really confused.

Chris: Ok, what is my favourite colour?

Both Scarlett and Vicky: White.

Chris: Which school do I go to?

Both Scarlett and Vicky: Lenz High.

Chris: My favourite sport?

Both Scarlett and Vicky: You like all of the sports you play.

Chris: Well, this is going to be hard.

Vicky: I am the real Scarlett, Chris! How can you possibly think that she is Scarlett? *(points at Scarlett)*

Chris: I know. Where did we inscribe 'best of friends' during the start of high school?

Vicky: On the first rock we climbed when we were kids. Ha! I got it! I am the real Scarlett!

Scarlett: No, we didn't inscribe that because the day we were going to do it, you went to the movies with Chia. It was your first date.

Vicky: NO! That's a lie!

Chris: It's not.

Vicky: NOOO!

Scarlett touches Vicky, and Vicky disintegrates. Scarlett runs to Chris.

Scarlett: Chris!

Chris: Scarlett! Oh my, I found you!
Scarlett: I didn't think I would ever find you.
Chris: What the heck is happening?
Scarlett: I have no idea, but we'll figure it out.

Chapter 17

THE RIDDLE

Chris and Scarlett head to the volcano as it is their only lead to finding the Figure. They talk about all the things that happened earlier. They try to understand what they are dealing with. Night falls, and they build a fire.

Scarlett: I'll go and find some fruits to eat.

Chris: I am coming with you.

Scarlett: I can look after myself.

Chris: I know you can, but I do not want to lose you again.

Scarlett smiles. They go and bring fruits that they know they can eat.

Chris: We cannot fall asleep at the same time.

Scarlett: Should we take shifts?

Chris: Sure. Shall I take the first shift?

Scarlett: No, I'll. I'm not that tired.

Chris: Ok, but wake me up when you want to sleep.

Scarlett: Ok.

Chris takes out his mat and goes to sleep. When he took out the mat, the paper he had picked up earlier falls out. Scarlett picks it up.

Scarlett (quietly to herself): Where did he get this?

She starts to worry because the paper looked very similar to the one she took from Jeanie. She brings out her part of the paper and tries to join them together. The two pieces of paper emit a golden light and both join together. It was like the paper had been never torn. She couldn't make out anything. She tried the old trick of bringing the paper to the fire, but to no avail. She becomes disappointed. After an hour or so, Chris wakes up and accidentally tips an open bottle of water on the paper.

Scarlett: Chris, are you okay?

Chris: Yeah, yeah, just a dream.

Scarlett realizes that the paper is soaking wet. Chris also sees it.

Chris: How did that paper become bigger?

Scarlett: Where did you get that paper?

Chris: It was in the basin in the cabin. I thought it might come in useful and took it, but how did it get bigger?

Scarlett: I had another piece of the paper. I found it in Ms Adam's (or whoever she was) hand. I tried to join them, and the paper started to emit a golden light. And then it was like the paper never ripped.

Chris: Did you try and…

Scarlett *(finishes his sentence)* Bring it to the fire? Yes, but it didn't work.

Chris: Darn, I am so sorry.

Scarlett: It's okay. It was of no use anyway.

She picks up the soaking paper and looks at it closely. When the firelight fell on the paper, words start to appear.

Scarlett: Chris!

Chris: What?

Scarlett: Letters!

The letters form as the map vanishes.

Chris *(reads out the letters)*: When two come together in the beginning-the waterfall and the volcano-good will rise.

Chris and Scarlett exchange confused looks.

Chris: What does that mean? Is that some kind of a riddle?

Scarlett: Our gems!

Chris: Your bracelet and my necklace!

Scarlett: This might have something to do with the letters.

Chris: Hey, you know, in math, when we have two numbers, and we have to find the average, we get one number right?

Scarlett: Yeah.

Chris: Now, if both numbers are exactly the same, their average is the same.

Scarlett: Right. What's your point?

Chris: Both our gems are exactly the same, and we have seen the waterfall and the volcano. Maybe the written text means that we need to go where both become one.

Scarlett: We need to get right under the centre point of the…

Both say: Volcano and the waterfall!

Scarlett: Should we go?

Chris: It's too dangerous in the dark. Let's wait for sunrise.

They wait until the sun is high in the sky and then try to find the centre point between the volcano and the waterfall.

Scarlett: Hold on.

Chris: What's wrong?

Scarlett: What if we find the centre point?

Chris: Yeah?

Scarlett: What will we do then? I mean, that will be the end of our search. I mean, we can't just dig until we find something.

Chris: Maybe the Figure has some 'on land' headquarters?

Scarlett: We would have known that if it had a lair. His lair must be below the ground.

Chris: Ok, but what should we do then?
Scarlett: Let's go to the waterfall. We haven't really investigated the waterfall. Maybe going there will give us some kind of clue.
Chris: Ok, let's go.

Their food supply was dwindling, so both of them just drank water from the lake. They finally reach the waterfall. It was huge and fell into a small, beautiful, clear lake. It was surrounded with a profusion of greenery and flowers.

Chris: Finally!
Scarlett: Let's take a break. Then we'll start searching for clues.

While Scarlett was taking in the beauty of the place, she notices a glimpse of the same golden light she saw when the pieces of paper joined together. It was coming from behind the waterfall.

Scarlett: Did you see that?
Chris: What?
Scarlett: That golden light behind the waterfall.
Chris: No.
Scarlett: Let's check it out.

They explore and find a way behind the waterfall.

Scarlett: Oh my gosh!
Chris: Woah, that was fun!
Scarlett: Fun? Almost being drenched by a waterfall is fun?
Chris: Yeah!

Scarlett shakes her head.

Chris: Look!

He points towards two hand imprints on the stone.

Scarlett: Woah! Should we try?
Chris: If this does something, it will be fantastic.

They place their hands on the imprints. The ground beneath them suddenly opens and they both fall into some kind of lair.

They land on something that looks very similar to stone, but feels like rubber. Chris and Scarlett get up and look around.

Chris *(whispers)*: Woah! What is this place?

Scarlett: Where the Figure lives!

Chapter 18

THE FIGURE

Scarlett and Chris try to calculate the distance and direction of the centre. When they do, they start walking to the centre. The passages they walk through are lit by fire, and the walls are made of glistening stone. They keep walking until they reach a fork in the path.

Scarlett: Damn!

They hear noises.

Chris: Stand back!

Chris and Scarlett go toward the sounds and spot the Figure. Their hearts begin to pound. The Figure looked like a human, very tall and strong. He wore some sort of brick red clothing with a large black cape with flames drawn on it.

The Figure: Christopher and Scarlett, welcome to my lair!

The moment he said lair, flames emerged from the ground.

Chris: YOU!

The Figure: 'You' has a name. Jargus.

Chris: Didn't ask for it.

Chris emotions get the best of him and he charges toward Jargus. He attempts to punch him, but Jargus uses his power and stops him in his tracks. Scarlett immediately realized that Jargus had telekinetic powers. Jargus uses those powers to lift up Chris and throw him across the 'room.'

Scarlett: CHRIS!

She runs to him, but Jargus stops her.

Jargus: You really think you could hurt me?! Ha-ha!

Chris summons all the energy he has and gets up.

Chris: WHERE ARE MY PARENTS?

Scarlett looks up and spots Chris' parents in a cage, hanging above the fire in the centre of the room.

Scarlett: Chris…

Chris looks at Scarlett, and then in the direction Scarlett is looking at and his face becomes pale.

Chris: MOM! DAD! CAN YOU HEAR ME?

Jargus: They can't hear you. They are unconscious, but not for long!

Chris: Let them down!

Jargus: Why should I? They have caused me harm. Now, give me your necklace.

Scarlett realizes why Jargus had come all those years back. He came to take the bracelet from her mom. And four months ago, he wanted the necklace from Chris' mom. But all the while, they had it. Scarlett realizes that the gems have some kind of power. And Jargus wants that power to complete whatever plan he had been formulating all these years.

Scarlett: Chris, don't give it to him.

Jargus: Now, now Scarlett, no one likes a know-it-all. This dimension needs a change. And finally, that change will be complete tonight.

Chris: Never!

Jargus is enraged. He magically increases in size to become less human. He reveals a long red sceptre and shoots Scarlett with a red concentrated flame. Scarlett falls down.

Chris: NO!

Chris runs toward Jargus and kicks him. Jargus flies in the air before landing flat on the ground.

Jargus: NO!

Screams in disbelief.

Jargus: You can't possibly be the one! Your parents…

Before Jargus could finish his sentence, Chris kicks him again, leading him into the fire. He stops himself using his sceptre. Jargus gets up and starts to fight with Chris. Chris punches Jargus again, but this time, fire shoots out of his hand. He begins to realize that he had powers too. It didn't make sense. It was a crazy idea, but it was all that he had to go on, so he tries to punch again. Chris uses his newly discovered powers as his defence, but ultimately Jargus beats him and Chris falls down. Scarlett opens her eyes and sees the fight. She tries to scream, but no sound comes out of her mouth. She tries to move, but can't. She tries to concentrate on her bracelet and her mind. This brought her soul back to peace. It binds with her bracelet and rises up from the ground. Water lifts her up. Her eyes turn ocean blue and water surrounds her, she moves her hand and controls the water. Jargus turns around.

Jargus: NO!!!

Jargus charges at Scarlett.

Scarlett: When two come together in the beginning – the waterfall and the volcano – good will rise.

Jargus immediately stops. It was as if saying those words gave her the power to stop him. She repeated that phrase while using her power against him. The water glowed as it cut through the air. The more she repeated the phrase, the stronger she became. Jargus used his sceptre to counter the water, but his power was inferior to Scarlett's. A blue ball started to emerge from her hands. She waits until the right time and then blasts Jargus. While that happened, Scarlett lowers down Chris' parents to the ground. Jargus exploded into tiny particles of water. Scarlett, drained of energy, falls to the ground.

Chris: Scarlett!

Chris gets up and runs to Scarlett. He tries to wake her up, but can't. He then runs to his parents. He opens the cage and unties them.

Chris: MOM! DAD!

Chris hugs them both.

Chris: Are you ok?

Chris' Mom: Honey, we are ok. Check on Scarlett.

Chris' Dad: Here, *(hands Chris an inch-long narrow bottle)* give her this.

Without question, Chris gives the liquid to Scarlett. He waits and waits. Nothing happens. Chris tears up, he holds her hand and pulls her into his lap.

Chris (quietly to Scarlett): Wake up, please.

Chris: No, no, no…

Scarlett wakes up with a gasp.

Chris: Oh Scarlett, Oh my gosh!

He hugs her tightly.

Scarlett: Is it over? Are your parents ok?

Chris nods, with tears in his eyes. He points to his parents. Scarlett smiles.

Chris: Mom, Dad, come!

Chris' Mom: Honey, we can't move

Chris: What?

Chris' Dad: Jargus took away our ability to move our legs.

Chris: No, no, no!

Footsteps are heard coming closer. They look over to the open arc, and see Mia and the team. She looks at them in disbelief. Half the team helps Chris' Mom and Dad, and the other half helps Scarlett and Chris.

Mia Adam: You did it!

Chris: We are starving!

Mia Adam laughs.

Scarlett: How did you…

She couldn't talk. She was drained of energy.

Mia Adam: Don't say anything. Just rest.

Everyone returns to the Exponent Course. The researchers can finally conclude the reason behind the high bursts of energy in places and undetected seismic activity. Many researchers are sent to the Jargus' lair for further research. Unfortunately, Chris' Mom and Dad are still paralyzed. They knew that this would happen to them. Chris still had faith. Aunt Claire visits Exponent Course for 2-3 weeks. When Scarlett and Chris are strong and healthy again, they resume their classes at the Exponent Course. Their story is shared worldwide and researchers from all over the world come to catch a glimpse of the site. Things are looking up for both Chris and Scarlett.

Scarlett: Can you believe it?

Chris: What?

Scarlett: It's all over.

Chris smiles, and gives her a kiss.

Chris: It's all over.

OR WAS IT?

DIMENSION

Chapter One

GOODBYE

Helene shouts from downstairs.

Helene: Alex, ready to go?

Alex: Could you spare five minutes?

Helene: Five minutes?

Alex: Just 5 minutes.

Helene: Ok, but only five minutes.

Alex then turns to her friend.

Alex: I am going to miss you so, so much!

Kara: I am going to miss you even more. I am going to miss going to school with you. I am going to miss your purple walls, the really messy dressing table that was there...

She points to the empty space in the room where the dresser used to stand.

Kara: I am going to miss that window, where we used to talk for hours on end.

Alex tears up and smiles as memories flash in her mind.

Kara: I am going to miss waking up and rushing to your house every Saturday. Ugh! Why do you have to go? Can't you like live with me?

Alex: I wish! I am going to miss everything here. This place will have a very special place in my heart always.

Kara: Hey, I wanted to give you this.

Kara hands Alex a small blue box.

Alex: What is it?

Attempts to open the box.

Kara: Don't open it here. Open it when you have time. I just want to give you this because this will keep our bond eternal and unbreakable. Keep it and never lose it.

Alex smiles and hugs Kara.

Alex: I will treasure it, no matter what!

Kara: Call me?

Alex: I'm gonna call you the minute I step into Bluestone.

Kara: I will be waiting.

Helene calls from downstairs.

Helene: Alex, Kara!

Alex: We are coming, Mom!

Kara and Alex hug one last time. They wanted to cherish this moment forever. They had been friends since they were babies. Their parents were friends in high school, and they were inseparable. This was the first time they were going to be separated from each other. They always knew that Alex would have to eventually go. They head downstairs. Their parents are exchanging goodbyes.

Tom (Kara's dad): You leaving now, huh?

Robert: So did you 10 years ago.

Tom: Yeah, and came back in two months!

Robert: Point to you.

Tom laughs and gives Robert a hug.

Tom: Visit!

Robert: It'll be like I never left.

Tom: Be safe, I'm serious.

Jenna: Gonna miss you!

Helene: Me too! Everything is happening too fast!

Jenna: Be safe!

Helene: I'll keep my eyes open.

Jenna and Helene hug.

Robert: It's time. We have to go.

Helene: Alex! Let's go!

Alex and Kara head to the car. Alex gets in. Kara's eyes well up. Robert and Helene get into the car. Alex rolls down the window. Kara runs to Alex's window.

Kara: Be safe and keep what's in the box at all times with you. Open the box in the car and don't keep it in any suitcase. Ok?

Alex: Sure. I'll miss you!

Kara: Miss you too!

Kara steps away from the car. Alex rolls up the window, and the car drives off. Alex opens the blue box Kara gave her. Inside is a ring with a teal gem set in it. She turned the ring around and saw a circle carved into the gem. She reckoned it was the company's brand. She put the ring on her finger. She suddenly felt something. She couldn't describe it. It was an unusual feeling that she had never felt before. It wasn't an emotional feeling. After about thirty minutes, they reached the airport. They checked in and then had their dinner.

Chapter Two

DOWN HILL

Helene: Boarding is in 25 minutes.

Helene and Robert look at each other. Alex could see that they were worried.

Alex: What's wrong?

Helene: Oh! Nothing, it's just that we are taking a big step in life. It's like a new chapter.

Alex: It's scary.

Robert: Just know that we are with you every step of the way, even if we aren't physically with you. Know that, always.

Robert and Helene always said that before a change, or when Alex was worried or nervous. The first time they ever said that to her she freaked out as it sounded like her parents were leaving her, but they assured that it was a thing they said to let her know that she will never be alone. She got used to them saying that, but when they said it this time, she tensed up a little. She got the same feeling she had when they first said this to her. They finish their dinner and board the plane. Alex had the window seat. The seat next to her was empty. Her parents sat behind her. As the plane starts to taxi for take-off, she surfed through her memories. She remembered all the happy moments, the hard times, and also when she felt safe. She watched a movie, and then fell asleep. She wakes up to find herself all alone. There was no one on the plane. She sits up, unbuckles her seatbelt and looks around. No one.

Alex: Mom? Dad?

Alex walks around the plane, looking for her parents. Or at least someone who could tell her what was going on.

Alex: Mom? Dad?

Her heart starts to pound faster. She wonders what to do. She runs to the window and looks out. All she sees is white, nothing else. She panics.

Alex: Alex, focus!

She organizes her thoughts by talking to herself.

Alex: You know that you are still flying, that means… that the pilot is still in the cockpit.

She runs towards the cockpit and sees two crew members. They appear shocked to see Alex.

Flight Crew member 1: How did you get on the plane?

Flight Crew member 2: That doesn't matter. Let's help her into a parachute.

The crew members grab another parachute and start helping Alex into it.

Alex: Wait! What is going on? Isn't the pilot in the cockpit?

Flight Crew member 1 *(While helping Alex into the parachute)*: We have absolutely no idea what is going on. The pilot is not in the cockpit. More questions when we land safely!

Flight Crew member 2: Now, you have to pull this string…

Flight Crew member 2: Count up to 5. Don't count fast, count at a slow pace like 1…2…3…4…5. Got It?

Alex: Yeah.

Alex's heart starts to pound even faster. She has no idea what is going on. She doesn't know where her parents are and now she has to jump off an airplane with apparently no pilot and no passengers. Both the crew members jump. Alex jumps right after because she doesn't want to land too far away from them. She closes her eyes against the blinding sun. She counts to 5 loudly and then pulls the string. She gasps when she feels the air brush against her as the parachute opens up. She calms down a little as she descends slowly. She is lucky enough to land on a plain surface. She frees herself from the parachute and looks around. She sees an empty road. The sun was almost straight above her so she assumed it was around 11 am. She starts to walk down the road, hoping to meet someone. Suddenly she heard people talking ahead of her. She increased her pace and saw the people who were talking. They were the same crew members from the aircraft.

Alex: Hey! Hello?

Alex increases her pace to a jog. The crew members turn around and stop when they see Alex.

Flight crew member 2: Hey! You made it!

Flight crew member 1: We thought you were lost.

Alex: I was. I just followed the road.

Flight crew member 1: Where did you land? On a tree?

Alex: No, thankfully, on plain ground. Sorry, uh… I don't know your name.

Flight crew member1: Jack.

Flight crew member 2: Alison. And you are?

Alex: Alex.

They start to walk together.

Alex: If you don't mind me asking, what on earth happened on that plane?

Alison: Honestly, we have no idea.

Jack: We were in the break cabin, waiting for our turn to be on call, when we realised that it was way past our duty time and no one had come in for their break. So we went out to check and saw that there were no passengers.

Alison: We first thought of notifying the captain. We thought the captain was still on the plane, considering that the plane was still in the air, but when we checked, there was no one in the cockpit!

Alex: Then how was the plane flying?

Alison: It was in auto-pilot mode!

Jack: It isn't surprising that we didn't crash into other planes.

Alison: We then thought jumping off the plane. We started to put on our gear and that is when we met you.

They continue to walk. Jack says it was probably around noon or 1 pm.

Jack: Alison, do you have water?

Alison: Yeah, picked two bottles from the pantry.

Alison hands Jack a water bottle.

Alison: Do you want some?

Alex: No, thanks.

Alex was thirsty but considering that they had only two bottles of water, she decided to wait a little longer before asking for any. It seemed like they had walked for hours. They took short breaks of about 15-20 minutes. They were just following the road. As sunset approached, they see a house.

Jack: Alison, look!

Alison: You think there is anyone there?

Jack: Only one way to find out. Plus, we need to find shelter. The sun is about to set.

Chapter Three

DISAPPEARANCE

They approach the house. The lights are on and they can hear people talking. They knock on the door. A middle-aged woman opens the door. Jack and Alison explain their situation to her. Alex remains silent. The woman, Elena, invites them in. There are three kids and Elena's husband Michael in the house.

Alison: We truly apologize for barging in.

Elena: Oh, don't worry. Be our guest. We are having a small get-together for the local residents. You can stay here. Now, could you please explain what happened?

Alison and Jack explain to Elena and Michael in detail what had happened to them. Jack, Alison and Alex feel that Michael and Elena didn't believe them.

Jack: It doesn't seem believable, but trust us, that is what happened.

Alison: Could you please direct us to the police? We could then, maybe contact our team back in Bronzeville.

Elena: Sure.

Elena takes them the nearest police station. It seems like they are on the outskirts of a city. Jack realises that they are at Bluestone, their flight's destination. They arrive at the police station. Elena tries to explain to the police officers what had happened to Alison, Jack and Alex. She bids them goodbye and leaves. The officers question them individually. The police ask Alex what was the last thing she remembered, how she got here. Alex felt that the police didn't believe her story. When the police ask her to wait outside, she looks around to see if she could find either Jack or Alison. She could not spot either of them. She concludes that they were probably still being interrogated. She sees something on the notice board. She goes. It was a missing person notice. For her. She turns pale. She is confused. A police officer sees her looking at the poster, and also what she was seeing. She took her to another room and asks her a few more questions. This officer was nicer that the previous one. She tries to find the person who had filed the missing person's report and found his picture. She showed the picture to Alex and she recognized the man. It was her uncle, her dad's brother and her godfather. She was even more confused. The police officer told her that her uncle had filed the missing person's report about four days ago. The plane carrying Alex and her family had crashed. There were two survivors and one missing. The police read out the description of the person who was missing. It matched Alex's description. Alex asked for the description of the other two survivors. Unfortunately, they weren't her parents. She came to the realisation that her parents were probably dead. She couldn't believe it. She didn't want to believe it. The police contacted her uncle and told her that he was on his way to the station. She asked the police officers if she could see Alison and Jack. The police said that she had come alone. Alex protested that she had come with two others. The police seemed to have no idea what she was talking about. Alex felt she was going crazy. Was her memory at fault? Her uncle arrived at the station.

Uncle Tim: Alex! Where have you been?! Oh my gosh! There was a huge search team looking for you. What happened? Wait, you know what, you need to relax. Why don't you rest in the car? I'll get us some food and we'll talk at home.
Alex: Ok.
Uncle Tim: What do you want to eat?
Alex: Anything.
Uncle Tim: You sure you don't want to pick?
Alex: I am sure.

Alex falls sleep in the car. She was exhausted from all that she had gone through. She was confused and terrified. They reach home around 9 pm. Uncle Tim shows her to her room. It was a guest room, but Uncle Tim told her that they would transform it into her room now that she would be living here permanently. Alex has no luggage or anything, except for the ring that Kara had given her. She asks Uncle Tim if she could make a call. She rings Kara. A stranger answers.

Unfamiliar voice: Hello?
Alex: Good evening! Could I please talk to Kara?
Unfamiliar Voice: Who?

Alex's heart dropped. She tried to push all the situations (of what could have happened to Kara) away.

Alex: Kara Holden?
Unfamiliar Voice: May I know who I'm speaking with?
Alex: Alex… Alex Adway.
Unfamiliar Voice: Oh my! You are alive! I saw the whole thing on the news. I am so sorry for your loss.
Alex: Uhhhh… thanks, but could I please talk to Kara Holden?
Unfamiliar Voice: Oh, you didn't know? The Holdens died in a terrible fire at the Plaza Mall.

Alex was speechless. Tears rolled down her cheeks.

Unfamiliar Voice: Hello?

Alex: Sorry, um, I know this is...um... weird to ask, but, when did this fire occur?

Unfamiliar Voice: Five months ago. Ma'am, are you ok?

Alex: Um... yeah, yeah, yeah, I am ok, sorry to disturb you.

Alex disconnects the phone. She feels numb with sadness. Her vision is blurred by tears. She couldn't think straight. She lost her parents and her best friend at the same time. She goes to her room. She can't stop her tears. She feels she is losing control of her life. She eventually falls asleep.

Uncle Tim *(enters Alex's room)*: Hey, dinner is on the table... oh, she is asleep.

Uncle Tim puts a blanket on her, turns off the lights and lets her sleep.

Chapter Four

SETTLING IN

The next morning.

Uncle Tim: Hey Alex! Got some sleep?

Alex: Yeah, sorry, I fell asleep. I know you had bought food.

Uncle Tim: It is ok, you were really exhausted. Here, I tried to turn yesterday's dinner into breakfast.

Alex: Thank you so much!

Uncle Tim: So, we need to go shopping for your room and some clothes, because you'll be staying here.

Alex: Oh, yeah…

Uncle Tim: I am so sorry for what happened to you, Alex. I wish I could bring your parents back. It is going to be hard, but with the right help, everything is going to be fine. I promise.

Tears run down Alex's cheeks. Uncle Tim comforts her. His eyes tear up as well as memories of his brother from their childhood flood his mind. Alex and Uncle Tim finish their breakfast and then head for the mall. Uncle Tim helps Alex pick furniture for her room, clothes and other necessary items. They then go to a therapist. Alex agrees because she was feeling that something was wrong with her. When Alex's session ended, she felt a little better as the therapist helped her deal with the death of her parents and Kara. Alex and Uncle Tim return home. Alex decorated her room and organized her things. She realised that her day had gone better than she had thought. Uncle Tim's support helped her through the dark times. She went for therapy all week. She knew that no one would believe what had happened to her. There was no evidence to support it and no witness. She decided to go with the idea that she had suffered temporary memory loss. She didn't take it to heart because she made it her life question (what had happened to her parents and all those people on the plane). Then she started going for therapy twice a week. School hadn't started yet, so she was at home all day while Uncle Tim went to work. He was a researcher/scientist. She had got the books she needed for the next semester and she studied, read books and played the piano. Gradually things got better for Alex. Since no one believed her, she knew that she would have to figure out what had happened by herself. She pretended to agree with what the therapist said about her parents' death. She was still sad but knew that crying about it was not going to help her. Her therapy sessions did help her adapt to her new life. She knew that her parents and Kara were always there with her, even if not physically.

Uncle Tim: Your school will start in three days. Let's get you some school supplies.

Alex: Alright!

At the mall.

Uncle Tim: So, we need Number 2 pencils, some pens, notebooks and any other things you think you might need.

Alex: Yup, let's start with the pens.

Alex and Uncle Tim finish shopping and head home.

Chapter Five

MOVING... AGAIN

Uncle Tim: Alex, I want to talk to you about something.
Alex: Yeah?
Uncle Tim: My team was looking at certain universe patterns and we noticed an unusual shift in our solar system. We have been trying to find out what that shift was and what caused it, but we haven't gotten anywhere. We know when it happened and for how long our solar system remained out of whack.
Alex: When did it happen?
Uncle Tim: The day I found you.
Alex: What?
Uncle Tim: listen, I know the therapist told you that your parents died in the plane crash and Kara died in the fire, and I don't want to confuse you or...
Alex: I know my parents didn't die in the plane crash.
Uncle Tim: What? I thought you said that you "kind of remembered" what had happened...
Alex: I know what I saw and what had happened. I said that because I knew that if I tried to argue, people would start to think that I am crazy. That is why I said I "kind of remember."
Uncle Tim: So, you do believe that something happened on the day you were coming here?

Alex: Yes… Something definitely happened during that time, but I'm not quite sure what.

Uncle Tim: We aren't too sure either. This is what I wanted to tell you. Oh and… I had completely forgotten… This project of trying to find out what caused the shift, needs my full attention.

Alex: You have to go?

Uncle Tim: Yeah, but don't worry, the school I enrolled you in is starting a new type of learning and teaching. It isn't very popular as we are trying to change the way students learn. You will be partnered with someone from your age group, from your class. And together, you will be participating in various competitions, courses and many other things.

Alex: So, you are sending me to boarding school?

Uncle Tim: No, no! It isn't exactly a boarding school. This course is like the continuation of a regular school. You will be in a whole different environment, nothing like boarding school. Of course, you will have designated rooms and you will have a class. You will just be living in a campus.

Alex: So… college?

Uncle Tim: Uhhhh… It is very hard to explain, but I will be there.

Alex: You will?

Uncle Tim: Well, your father was one of the original co-founders of this board.

Alex: Really?

Uncle Tim: Yes, that is why you guys were moving here. Your father tried to incorporate the foundation in Brownstone. But the city didn't respond too well to the idea, so he tried to pitch the idea here, and when the people here responded well to the project, he decided to transfer here. He enrolled you in X-Squared, the school. I was also in on the project, and helped him carry it out when he was still in Brownstone. Your father's aim was to change the school's teaching system. So, he did a lot of research on study patterns, reasons for success rates, etc. He knew that attending school was very important for a child's development, but in order to change the system, he made a new course, which is learning about team building, how to be independent, and how to earn a living at a young age. He divided his idea into two parts-one called the X-Squared Change in Time programme.

Alex: X-Squared? Is that the school's name?

Uncle Tim: Ha-ha! Your father wasn't the one to make up cool school names, but since he was a child, he dreamed of the school we went to being named X-Squared or 2 Root 2. He loved math.

Alex laughs.

Alex: He sure did… that sounds like something Dad would say.

Uncle Tim: So, X-Squared was where a child will come to school in the morning and leave in the afternoon, quite like a normal school, except the courses will be different. The second part-called X-Cubed Ideal change in Prospective programme.

Alex: Hahaha! Now that is clever.

Uncle Tim gives a warm smile as memories of his brother and him flash in his mind for a split second. He could see Robert in Alex.

Uncle Tim: Has anyone told you that you are just like Robert?

Alex smiles.

Uncle Tim: X-Cubed is a type of boarding school. Many

parents leave their kids in boarding school, and the student's end up hating the experience because of bullying, insecurity and mean elders at the campus. Your father wanted to change that, so he created a boarding school that encouraged team building, independent living and was very different from the usual boarding schools. He successfully carried out this project. Branches of the school were opened in many cities across the country. Robert took a two-year extension because he didn't want to leave Brownstone, but he eventually had to because it was hard for him to manage all the schools through video conferences and two-day visits.

Alex: He had been doing this for three years?

Uncle Tim: Yeah.

Alex: How come he never told me?

Uncle Tim: He didn't?

Alex: He only said that it was a "project" he was working on.

Uncle Tim: Maybe he didn't want to let anyone suspect that there was a chancc of him leaving. I think he was hoping that he could open a branch in Brownstone, but when his attempts failed, he finally decided to come here.

Alex: So, if my parents were still alive, we would be living here, and I would go to the Change in Time programme?

Uncle Tim: When your father passed away, the foundation committee that Robert had created, agreed to run the foundation together instead of having just one person in charge.

Alex: You are part of the committee?

Uncle Tim: Yup.

Alex: And that is why you have to stay here? For the project you are working on?

Uncle Tim: You guessed right. I know you may want some

time to decide if you wanna come with me or go attend Change in Time… but you have three days to figure it out.

Alex: I want to come with you.

Uncle Tim: You are sure? I mean you have three days to think it through.

Alex: I've decided. I think attending Ideal Change of Prospective programme would be good and I'd rather stay with you than alone.

Tim smiles at her.

Uncle Tim: Ok then, I'll give you the list of things you'll need for school. You can organize your things. We will start packing tomorrow.

Alex: Ok, umm… I just wanted to ask, before we leave for X-Cubed, could we go to an ice-cream shop?

Uncle Tim knows why Alex wants to go to the ice-cream shop. Her father's birthday was the day after and he loved ice cream. Uncle Tim used to take Robert to an ice-cream shop every year for his birthday when they were kids.

Uncle Tim: Sure, kiddo.

Chapter Six

THE ICE CREAM SHOP

The next day.

Uncle Tim: Ready to go?

Alex: Yeah.

Tim and Alex go to an ice-cream shop. Every year, on his birthday, Robert would insist on going for an ice-cream. As they drove there, Alex remembered the last time she went to the ice-cream shop with her parents. They had gone there very late. Her dad was hoping that the shop would be open.

Alex's flashback.

Robert: I really hope an ice-cream shop is open.

Helene: We'd be lucky if we found one. It's pretty late.

Alex: Why did you have to go to work today? It is your birthday. You could have taken the day off.

Robert: I know, but I had to go to work. It was necessary.

Helene: Found One!

Robert: Let's pull up.

Helene: Oh! I think he is closing his shop.

Robert: Hurry!!

The pull up to the ice-cream shop.

Robert: Hi! I know you are probably closing, but could you make an exception for us?

The ice-cream vendor: Ahhh... sure... What would you like?

Robert: I want chocolate ice-cream.

Alex: Same here.

Helene: Vanilla.

The ice-cream vendor: Would you like it in a cone or a cup?

Robert: Cone.

Alex: Cup.

Helene: Cone, please.

The ice-cream vendor starts to get their order ready. Robert, Helene and Alex step away from the vendor.

Robert: Finally!

Alex: Finally, indeed! What was so urgent and important that you had to go to work today, and come back later than usual, Dad?

Robert: There were many meetings today, and I had to finish up some work.

Alex: We almost missed your birthday ice-cream.

Robert: But we didn't. I am so happy!

Helene: We can see it.

All of them laugh.

Helene: How was school, honey?

Alex: It was ok. Nothing much happened. Just the usual.

Helene: Did you get any homework?

Alex: Yeah, but it has to be handed only two weeks later.

Helene: You should work on it tomorrow. You should not procrastinate.

Alex: But then Kara and I won't get the chance to sleepover.

Helene: Who said that? Think about it. If you finish your work and she finishes hers, you could have a sleepover where you actually do fun things instead of studying.

Alex: I guess so.

Robert: Our ice-creams are ready!

They go to the vendor and get their ice-creams.

Alex's flashback ends.

Uncle Tim: We are here.

They both go into the shop and get chocolate ice-cream.

Uncle Tim: Happy Birthday to your father!

Alex: Happy birthday to Dad!

They finish their ice-cream and return home to finish packing. Alex packs all that she thinks she would need. She doesn't know what is about to happen or how things will turn out, but one thing she does know: this will be a new chapter in her life. She also hopes to find out what happened to her parents and all those other passengers on that plane. The fact that Uncle Tim believes her story, gives her confidence and a sense of security. She feels ready to handle any obstacles that she might encounter. She keeps her family's photo in her suitcase and zips it closed. She took a shower and then opened the window of her room. A light breeze blows in. From the corner of her eye, she thought she saw her ring glow. She looks at it. But it wasn't glowing. "What if the ring is the reason I survived the supposed plane crash?" Maybe if she takes off the ring, she might be able to be with her parents. If the ring was the thing that saved her, then she'd rather not wear it. As she starts to take it off, she remembered what Kara had said. She pushes the ring back on her finger. There was a reason why she was still here and she will not leave until she fulfils her purpose, she tells herself. She eventually goes to sleep.

Chapter Seven

THE WHITE LINE

The next day.

Uncle Tim: Good morning!

Alex: Good morning!

Uncle Tim: One day before school. Excited?

Alex: I always forget how alike you and my dad are.

Tim laughs.

Alex *(laughing)*: You know, he always used to say that the day before school re-opened. I am ready for whatever is in store for me.

Uncle Tim: That's the spirit… So, I still have to go to work. There are pancakes in the blue casserole, and you know where the syrup is.

Alex: Yup, thank you!

Uncle Tim leaves for work. Alex finishes her breakfast and then takes a shower and cleans her room. She makes sure that all the things she needed for school are packed. She didn't have much left to do. She goes downstairs. Maybe she will clean the house. The living room looked a little messy. She cleans the living room, the kitchen and then the entry way. It was about noon by the time she was done. She watched some TV, read, and then made herself something to eat. Then she went outside.

She observed a white line across the sky. It couldn't have been a cloud, because clouds couldn't be so perfect and defined. The line was solid in colour, and didn't look like it had a cloudy texture. She tried to see where the line ended, but couldn't. She decides to take a picture to show Uncle Tim when he returned. But the line wasn't there in the picture. She clicked again, but still the line wasn't visible in the image. She went back into the house. Uncle Tim returned for dinner.

Alex: I wanted to tell you something.

Uncle Tim: Yeah what's up?

Alex: I might sound crazy, but when I was on the porch today, I saw a very fine and clear white line across the sky. It didn't look like a cloud.

Uncle Tim: Did you take a picture?

Alex: That's the thing. I tried to take a picture, but the white line wasn't visible in the image. I tried to take its photo many times, but the white line was not visible.

Uncle Tim: That's unusual.

Alex: I know, right?

Uncle Tim: Maybe something was obscuring your sight? So it looked like a clear white line in the sky or it could be something that is inexplicable.

Alex: I thought about the light interfering with my sight. So, I walked around to see if I could see the white line from elsewhere.

Uncle Tim: And?

Alex: I could see it from everywhere.

Uncle Tim: Then I am not sure what it could be. Don't stress yourself about it. There are just some things that we humans cannot process or explain.

Alex: I guess.
Uncle Tim: Oh, I wanted to tell you that a bus will take you to X-Cubed along with the other students of your grade.
Alex: When will you come?
Uncle Tim: I'll be there. I'll come and visit you when you have settled in your room.
Alex: Promise?
Uncle Tim: Promise!

They finish their dinner and go to bed.

Chapter Eight

THE JOURNEY

Alex: When will the bus be here?
Uncle Tim: In about 15 minutes.
Alex: I'll carry my suitcases down.
Uncle Tim: Should I help you with that?
Alex: No, it's ok.
Uncle Tim: Come down quickly. Your breakfast is ready.
Alex: Ok.

Alex carries down her suitcases down the stairs.

Uncle Tim: ALEX!!
Alex: What happened?
Uncle Tim: I didn't check my email yesterday, but there are some more items that you will need to take to school.
Alex: Oh, umm, what are they? We still have about 12 minutes left.
Uncle Tim: Eat your breakfast and I'll bring them.
Alex: I can multitask. What are the items?
Uncle Tim: Well, they are items of furniture.
Alex: Items of furniture? For what?
Uncle Tim: To place in your room. So, there is… Oh, I didn't read the last part, my bad.
Alex: What does it say?

Uncle Tim: The student is to pick out any furniture (not anything big) to put in their bot… your room… our services will come in later and pick them up to avoid the hassle of packing the furniture. A bed with a mattress and sufficient blankets are provided.

Alex: So, I just have to pick the furniture?

Uncle Tim: Yup, I am so sorry for panicking.

Alex: No no-it's all good!

Alex goes upstairs and chooses the items of furniture she wants to take. As she is finishing her breakfast, she hears a vehicle approach the house. She looks out the window and sees a small titanium white bus with dark, Prussian blue stripes along the bottom. It is the cleanest bus she had ever seen. The windows were tinted, and you could see your reflection on the bus's surface. Alex ran out.

Uncle Tim: Your bus is here.

Alex: I saw. It's so clean!

Uncle Tim laughs. They carry out Alex's suitcases, and load them onto the bus.

Uncle Tim: Good luck! I'll meet you there.

Alex: Thank you!

Uncle Tim: You have my phone number, right?

Alex: Yeah, I do.

Alex's voice cracks with nervousness. She didn't know what was ahead of her. She was shy of talking to strangers. Unlike Kara, who was the friendlier of them. She only liked to talk to her parents.

Uncle Tim: Don't be nervous. Everything is going to be okay. I'm here. And you are going to have fun.

Alex: I hope so.

The bus doors open.

Uncle Tim: Hey Nigel!

Nigel, the bus driver: Good morning, sir!

Uncle Tim: Bye Alex!

Alex: Bye!

Alex steps into the bus. The students are chattering to each other. She looks around. The whole bus is packed even though there are only around 11 students. She looks for a vacant seat. There is only one that is free, a window seat. On the adjacent seat was a boy with black hair, curly in the front and straight at the back. He had brown eyes and was quite tall. He was wearing a brown coat and sneakers. She gathers up the courage to walk to the seat. Thankfully, before she could excuse herself, the boy makes place for her to go to the window seat. Once she sits down, she takes out her phone and starts listening to her music.

Boy sitting next to Alex: Hey! Are you new around here?

Alex: Umm… yeah, is it that noticeable?

Boy: No, no! It's just that I haven't seen you in school. So, I assumed that you are new.

Alex: You assumed right. I just moved here.

Boy: From where?

Alex: From Brownstone.

Boy: Oh! I used to live there when I was a kid. Until I came here to boarding school.

Alex didn't know how to respond to that. She didn't want him to think that she was snooping.

Boy sitting next to Alex: My parents are world travellers. They help patients who can't afford medical care.

Alex: Oh wow! That's amazing. I don't mean the people

lacking medical care-I mean your parents.

The boy laughs.

Alex: I... uh... didn't get your name.

Boy: Darren.

Alex: Alex.

Darren: Well, let me start again. Hi Alex! My name is Darren. How are you doing today?

Alex laughs, then plays along.

Alex: Hello, Darren! I am doing fine. How about you?

Darren: Quite well.

Both start laughing.

Darren: So, why did you move here, and why this school? I thought I saw your dad waving you goodbye. Or maybe my eyes are playing tricks on me and I couldn't get a clear picture.

Alex: That was my uncle. I moved here cause my dad got a job here. Well, he had his job, but he had to move here. It's complicated to explain. I was going to go to X-Squared, but now I'm going to X-Cubed.

Darren: Oh, well, I hope boarding school is a good experience. It is, at least according to the school's motto.

Alex: You don't go to X-Cubed?

Darren: No, yes, kind of. I went to its junior programme, this is the senior programme.

Alex: Ohhh…

Alex feels she should have researched about the school more. She would feel closer to her dad too.

Darren: The senior programme is at a different centre, so it is like it's my first time at school.

Alex: Right… so all these are your classmates?

Darren: No, they aren't. They are students from other schools.

I thought I'd meet at least a few of my classmates here from the junior programme, but there is no one I know.

Alex: How is the experience at boarding school? Be honest.

Darren: Ha-ha! It's actually pretty good. Robert Adway really knew what he was saying.

Alex smiled when she heard her father's name. Memories of her dad flashed before her.

Darren: You may not know him. He wasn't big on press or media. He was a reserved person. Not many people know anything about his family. All we know is that he has a brother, Timothy Adway. He was married and had a daughter. Or was it a son. People really don't know. He was a very private person. Anyway, he was someone who wanted to create a better school, with a whole different way of learning. When I first heard of his project, I thought it was cool, but I knew he would be criticized for it. He was. But then the criticism ended once the programme was running and people liked the system. Robert Adway was a genius, and because of him, many students have a great experience at boarding school. At least, I've had a good experience. Let me change that, the best experience.

Alex: Really? That makes me less nervous for sure.

Darren: Don't be nervous. If the junior programme was so good, the senior programme can only be better.

Alex: I'll try not to be nervous.

Nigel: Guys, there is way too much noise on the bus. Please, tone it down.

Chapter Nine

X-CUBED

Alex listens to her music and looks out the window. She starts reading the X-Cubed guide Uncle Tim sent her when she realised that she didn't really know anything about the school she was going to and requested it. Alex couldn't believe that her dad had created all this. It made her so happy that he had accomplished so much. But it also made her sad that he "disappeared" just when things were getting better. They reached X-Cubed. Alex was amazed by the school buildings. They were huge and the whole area was like a small campus. The structures were like office buildings. They had blue tinted windows, with a white stripe around the top. They looked beautiful. Her nerves became calmer when she realised that she would be in a place that her dad had created.

Darren: Woah! That is sick!

Alex: It is stunningly breathtaking!

Darren: You can say that again.

Nigel: Take your luggage, and then follow the blue carpet to the door. There you will meet your senior X-Cubed principal.

Everyone rushes to get their luggage. Alex waits patiently until everyone has their luggage, and then gets her own.

Alex: Thank you, Mr Nigel!

Nigel: You are very welcome, young lady. You look just like your father.

Alex smiles at him.

Alex: Will I be seeing you around?

Nigel: Yes, you will. I am the sports instructor.

Alex looks surprised. She hadn't expected the sports teacher to also drive the bus.

Nigel: Shocked?

Alex: No, no! It's just that…

Nigel: All the teachers drive their new students to the school on their first day. It's a community exercise.

Alex: It's a very good thing.

Nigel: You might want to run along. Your class is almost next to the gate.

Alex looks behind her and realises that almost everyone has gone into the building.

Alex: Oh, yeah! Thank you, again!

Nigel smiles at her. She runs to join the others.

Darren: Where were you? I thought you were lost.

Alex: Just getting my luggage.

They enter through a black glass gate. All of the students start to chatter about how the place looks. It was like they had entered the next century. There was a big screen above them. In front of them was a small stage with a mic stand. The walls were painted white and the ceiling was very high. The room was circular and well-lit thanks to the huge windows. There were rectangular lights dangling from the ceiling. All the students quieten down as they see a woman walk onto the stage and approach the mic.

The woman on the mic: Welcome, students, to X-Cubed!

The students start to cheer and clap.

The woman on the mic: I am Larrison Edwards, head of X-Cubed. Hope you have had a good journey here. This will be your home for your senior programme, and all the teachers here, staff and myself, will ensure that you have the best educational experience, filled with knowledge, happiness and most of all, fun. You are now entering a very different programme. Those of you who have attended the junior programme, you do have a list of what you will be learning, but this programme is very, very different. It is more challenging, and it offers more insight than usual into things. Our school approaches learning in ways that will ensure the earth's sustainability. We also stress on new technologies as the future of learning, while taking the good from older learning techniques. Unfortunately, the man behind this master project, Robert Adway, passed away in a plane crash.

Alex's heart filled with sadness, she really missed her parents.

Larrison Edwards: Let us observe a minute of silence to honour Robert Adway, while a slideshow that was meant to be part of his biography, plays on the screen.

There is pin-drop silence in the whole room. Pictures of Robert Adway appeared on the screen. There were pictures of him at charity events, meetings, the day he finalized the projects. Alex had seen these pictures, but she never knew what they were for. The last picture was of his family, the photo they had taken the day before they left for Bluestone, the day before the aircraft incident. Tears fill Alex's eyes. She tries to blink them away as fast as she can. She noticed people from her bus look towards her. Darren looked at her, confusion writ large on his face. He had not known that he was sitting next to the daughter of

Robert Adway.

Larrison Edwards: His family is in our prayers.

She looks at Alex and then looks away.

Larrison Edwards: The senior programme is different from the junior programme. We have classified all of you in different class sections. Your classmates are the people you were on the bus with. We have further classified you. You will be with a partner through the senior programme. If there is any reason that you do not want to be with the partner assigned to you, please take it up with us, but it is highly recommended that you try and create a strong relationship with your partner. It is a very important social aspect of life, learning how to make prompt connections and how to communicate. Your partner is the person who was sitting next to you on the bus.

Alex and Darren look at each other and smile. They were relieved that they were partners as they were comfortable with each other.

Larrison Edwards: There are four sections, hence four buildings. Each section will be allotted a building. Each pair will have one floor to themselves and they will work with another pair as a study group. Some may say that giving two students a whole floor is not a good use of space. But the floors have common lounge areas where the students will study together. There is a gym and gardens on one of the two floors. The cafeteria is where you will have your breakfast, lunch and dinner. You will not be allowed to take your breakfast, lunch or dinner to your bots, but there will be snacks provided in the cafeteria, which you can choose to take to your bots. Oh-I almost forgot, your bots are your rooms. We use the term bots. You will be taken to your floors by a teacher or a staff member.

They are standing there (*points to the line of teachers and staff members who weren't there when Ms Larrison had started her speech).*

Larrison Edwards: Each teacher is holding a pair's name and the section you will be in. Once again, welcome to X-Cubed, I am Larisson Edwards.

The students clap and each tries to find the section and partner.

Darren: I had no idea you were Alex Adway. You never told me.

Alex: You never asked.

Darren: Don't try to be clever. I am so sorry for your loss.

Alex: Uh… thanks? I don't really know how to respond to that. I haven't really talked to many people haha.

Darren smiles at her.

Darren: You are doing good. Now, are you excited or what?

Alex: I am excited. Oh, there are our names.

Alex points to a lady holding a sign with their names. Alex could see people looking at her. She knew they were looking at her because she was Robert Adway's daughter.

Darren: Ignore them.

Lady holding the sign: Hi, guys! Are you Darren Adams and Alex Adway?

Darren: Yes, we are.

Lady holding the sign: I am Linda Johnson, the Skills teacher. I will be taking you guys to your floor and to your bots. Follow me.

Linda leads them outside the building, to a big garden, with luscious green grass, a cute pathway and benches. Surrounding the garden were campus buildings. There were two tall buildings on the right and the left, and in front was a wide building almost as tall as the other four buildings. The wide building were like two separate buildings, connected by a bridge of some sort.

Linda: This is your campus.

Darren: It is huge!

Linda: It is. The building to your right is called Prosperity, the one next to it is called Peace. The building to your left is called Change and the one next to that is called Future. Their names don't classify students or anything, they are just names. The building in front of you is called the Centre. Do you notice the bridge?

Darren and Alex *(in unison)*: Yeah.

Linda: That separates the building to left and right wings. Prosperity and Peace will carry out their courses in the right wing, and Change and Future in the left wing. Each floor in each building is the same. Your room is in Prosperity.

Linda takes them into the Prosperity building. The ground floor seemed like a lounge area and a reception. Linda says something to the receptionist and then leads Darren and Alex to a wall. Darren and Alex exchange confused glances. Linda presses a point on the wall, and wall breaks apart. Alex gasps. She thought the wall was collapsing. But the walls open to reveal an elevator.

Darren: Whoa, how on earth did that happen?

Linda: It is one of the new features of the building. Your floor is number 7.

Darren: Floor number 7? That is really high up!

Linda: Are either of you afraid of heights?

Darren and Alex: Nope.

Linda: Good.

Linda presses the 7th floor button. The elevator doors close and it is all dark.

Darren: Uhhhh… are the lights not working?

Linda: Wait and see.

Alex and Darren hear a sound very similar to a machine. A light comes on behind them. They turn around to see that they are in a glass elevator. They could see outside the building. They could also see how high up they were going. Alex's eyes begin to glow with excitement.

Darren: Whoa!... aren't we going really high?

Linda: The 7th floor is the highest floor.

Darren: Is it the best floor to be on or the least good floor to be on?

Linda: You'll find out.

The elevator stops smoothly and silently. The doors of the open into a room that was dome-shaped. Looking up they could see the sky. It was like there was no ceiling. There was a glass door across the room leading to what looked like a balcony. The lights were dim and appeared to come from the floor. There was light brown carpeting, the walls were a matt light whitish brown. In the middle of the room there was a staircase leading below. To the right of the staircase were a sofa and a coffee table. It was quite cozy. Alex and Darren looked around in wonder, trying to take it all in.

Linda: Welcome to your floor!

Alex and Darren remain silent.

Linda: You guys ok?

Darren: Just speechless.

Alex: This is 'our' floor?

Linda: Yes.

Alex: It is so beautifully designed! The colors give it a calm and cozy atmosphere and it feels like home. This is incredible. It's… I can't find the right words to describe it.

Darren: What is that pole with the metal bars around it for?

Points to the pole a little further away from the staircase.

Linda: It is a pole you guys can use to slide down. There are stairs as well, if you guys aren't comfortable using the pole.

Darren: This is the coolest floor in the building.

Linda: Alex, your room is… let me see... ah – your room is 305, and Darren, your room is 306.

Points to the two doors on the floor.

Linda: Why don't you guys drop off your luggage and then I'll show you where everything is. You can ask for a map but the school recommends that the students find a way of remembering their way around.

Darren: Thanks!

Alex: Give us a minute.

Linda: Here are your cards. This will enable access to your rooms, the cafeteria and other places. Don't lose it.

Alex: Thank you!

Alex and Darren go to their rooms. Alex looks around her room. It was plain with a single bed placed against the left wall. The bed was high above the ground. Alex loved it! She opened the curtain near the bed and found ample storage space. The room was spacious and furnished with a television mounted on the wall. There was a big window opposite of the door. To the left of the main door was a small door that led to the bathroom. There was a built-in cupboard next to the television. There was a glass desk to the right of the television. Alex's eyes brightened. She was so excited to arrange her room, with the side table, chair and mini bookshelf she had picked up at Uncle Tim's. She put her luggage on the floor, took a notepad and pen out of her bag to take notes. She left the room. She met Darren coming out of his room.

Darren: Are you ready?

Alex: Yeah. The rooms are…

Darren: Bots.

Alex: Right. The bots are amazing.

Darren: I know! Especially the light coming from the lower ends of the bots.

Alex: Let's go.

Darren: Wait, we don't know how we are going to remember all the other places.

Alex: I have my notepad. We will organize them by floor, door and place name.

Darren: Great! Let's go.

Linda: You guys ready?

Darren and Alex in unison: Yup!

Linda: Firstly, there is a gym on this floor that you, along with the pair on the floor below, will be using. There are also teachers' rooms here, but they are sound-proof. So it's like they aren't even here.

Darren: Where is the gym?

Linda: Do you see that small black board there, on the wall next to the sofa?

Darren: Yeah.

Linda: If you swipe your card there, the door to the gym will open.

Alex: And where are the teachers' rooms?

Linda: Their doors are hidden. You won't be able to see them.

The teachers wanted a place where they wouldn't be disturbed by the students, so they have rooms that are not easily visible. Now, we will go to the cafeteria and then work our way towards all the other places you need to know about.

They leave the Prosperity building and go to the Centre. Linda showed them the cafeteria, the various classrooms, the big gym, sports courts, garden, the library and the swimming pool. Alex and Darren were feeling overwhelmed. The school was amazing. Linda left them to find their way back to their floor. Alex and Darren didn't find their way back. They met the two other people living on the floor below. The two other students were Jade and Jaden. The four of them talked for two hours about the school, how they could organize study meetings etc. Alex and Darren went back to their floor to unpack and arrange their room. Alex took a quick shower. It was dinner time by then. Alex and Darren went to the 6th floor to ask if Jade and Jaden were going to dinner and when. Jade and Jaden didn't know either, but then they all got an email with their time-tables. They had to be at dinner at 7 pm. The four of them met up on the ground floor. Darren and Alex introduced themselves to the other students. They all made their way to the cafeteria for dinner. There were a wide variety of food. The cafeteria was huge. It was not meant only for the students. There were teachers, many officers and scientists too. Alex looked for Uncle Tim, but she couldn't find him. Alex and Darren left together after dinner. When they reached the Prosperity building, they saw Uncle Tim.

Alex: Uncle Tim!

Alex ran towards Tim.

Uncle Tim: Hey! How was your first day? Hi, Darren!

Darren was star struck when he saw Tim, who was now the co-owner of the organization. He was surprised that Tim knew his name.

Darren: H…hello Mr Adway.

Alex: This place is amazing. I can tell that dad designed it.

Uncle Tim: It epitomises all his dreams, doesn't it? I am going to be at the research centre, so I will not be able to see you much, but I will text and call you every day. Tell me a time when you'll be free to call.

Alex: Is 9 pm ok?

Uncle Tim: Great! Well, sleep well. Get some rest both of you. You have a long day ahead of you tomorrow.

Alex: Ok, bye!

Uncle Tim: Bye, guys!

Uncle Tim goes towards the main building.

Darren: It was nice meeting your uncle.

Alex: He is all I've got now.

They go up to their rooms. In the next few weeks, the students were busy with many activities other than academics-sports, cooking, gardening, skills they would need later in life like paying the bills, etc. The students had to work hard in order to get good grades. Alex spent a lot of her free time in the library and her study times with Darren, Jade and Jaden. She and Darren would often go to the basketball courts in the evening. Alex was enjoying everything, but she still hadn't found out what had happened to her parents. She asked Uncle Tim about it, but he said that the team didn't have any leads either.

Chapter Ten

GETTING IT OUT OF THE SYSTEM

One month later. Alex wakes up early. She couldn't go back to sleep, so she went to the balcony. Darren joins her there.

Darren: Hey!

Alex *(startled)*: H...Hey!

Darren: I didn't mean to startle you. What are you doing up so early?

Alex: Couldn't sleep. And you?

Darren: Was finishing up the essay. Did you finish yours?

Alex: Yeah.

Darren: What were you staring at?

Alex: The stars.

Darren: What is so interesting about them?

Alex: There are billions of stars in the sky, and at least half of them have a solar system. Imagine if life existed out there... technology isn't advanced enough to know if they are there.

Darren: That is cool to think about. Hey, if you don't mind me asking, how did your parents pass away? I mean, only if you are comfortable talking about it.

Alex: Well, we were coming here, and then I guess the plane crashed and they died. I was one of the survivors.

Darren: You know, the day of the plane crash, something

weird happened.

Alex: What?

Alex was hoping for something. She didn't know what, but something.

Darren: The sky was white for like five minutes, and it wasn't like cloud white, it was a rich white. I tried to take a picture to show it to my friends, but it didn't come out in the photo. Neither was it visible to my friends. I didn't think of it much.

Alex remembered the time she saw the white line across the sky.

Darren: You think I'm crazy.

Alex: No, I don't. Seriously. I'm going to tell you something that will make you think that I am crazy, but it was real, and it really happened.

Darren: Lets hear it.

Alex: Again, bear in mind that what I'm about to tell you is unbelievable, and you may think I am going crazy.

Darren: Just say it.

Alex: Ok. So, you know that everyone thinks my parents died in a plane crash and that I was a survivor?

Darren: Yeah.

Alex: That is not what I remember. I used to live in Brownstone and we were moving here because of Dad's job. I remember the day vividly. I spent the day with my best friend Kara, and then we left for the airport. We boarded the plane and then we were in the air. I fell asleep while watching a movie. When I woke up, there was no one on the plane-literally no one. I looked outside the window, and we were still flying. At that point I started to panic, and I looked around desperate to find someone, anyone. Luckily, I found two crew members ready to jump off the plane with a parachute. They told me that the pilot was missing, and that they didn't know what was going on either. They helped me into a parachute and we jumped off the plane. Once on the ground, we tried to find a place to ask for shelter or at least to find out where we were. We found a very kind family, who then took us to the police station. The police asked us questions individually. It had been at least an hour since I had seen any of the other crew members. Then, while I was waiting for a police officer, I saw a missing person's poster… of me. It was the craziest thing. An officer tracked down the person who had filed the missing person's report-and it was Uncle Tim who had done so. I then asked about the delayed flight that I was on. We were supposed to land at 4 pm. They informed me that there were no delayed flights. I started to panic even more. They then told me that I was a survivor of the plane crash that had happened five days before my arrival at the police station. I was so confused. I tried to tell them what had actually happened to me, but they didn't believe me. I heard them telling Uncle Tim that I should probably see a doctor because I must have hit my head hard and was coming up with these stories. I tried to call Kara and tell her about what had happened, and if she knew what was going on. I called her number, and found out that she had died in a fire… FIVE MONTHS AGO. I was terrified. I did not know what was going on. The therapist Uncle Tim took me to did help me deal with the death of my parents and best friend, but she couldn't convince me that I was a survivor of a plane crash. What had happened to me was real, and I remember every bit of it-second by second. I pretended as if I believed her, but I knew that that wasn't the case.

Alex takes a deep breath. She was glad and relieved that she let it all out. She was happy it was with Darren-she felt comfortable with him

Alex: I've been trying to find a clue to what could have happened, but I have gotten nowhere.

Darren: Wow, Alex, I didn't know, I am so sorry that all this happened to you.

Alex: You believe me?

Darren: Honestly, at first, it wasn't believable, but you told me about this in such detail, it can't be false. It is still hard to believe, but I trust you.

Alex: Really?

Darren: Yeah.

Alex smiles. Darren gives her a hug.

Alex: It's a relief to get it out of my system.

Darren: Our one-week holiday is coming up. We can go to the cinema. Want to go to see the new Defenders movie?

Alex: That would be great!

The holidays came along and Alex and Darren got permission to go to the nearest mall to see a movie. They book their tickets for the Defenders, and then waited for the day.

Chapter Eleven

THE MOVIES

The day of the movie.

Darren: We will leave at 4 pm.

Alex: Ok. Are Jade and Jaden coming?

Darren: I asked them, but they said that they have some sort of video game marathon today… I didn't quite understand.

Alex: Basically, they play one competitive video game for the whole day. They planned it last week.

Darren: It's like they are making up for all the days they couldn't play video games.

Alex: That is exactly right.

Darren: Oh!

Around 3.30 pm, Alex knocks on Darren's door.

Darren: Let's go!

Alex: What if we get lost? I mean, we are going to a place that we have never gone to before.

Darren: We will be fine. We have our GPS and they can track us if we get lost. This will also earn us independence points.

Alex: I just hope we don't get lost.

Darren: If we do, we have music to keep us company while walking.

Alex smiles. They reach the movie theatre.

Darren: Do you have our tickets?

Alex: Yup.

Darren: On your phone?

Alex: Yeah.

They approach the receptionist at the cinema.

Receptionist: Hello, which movie would you like to watch?

Alex: The Defenders. We already bought the tickets. Here they are.

Alex shows her phone with the digital tickets.

Receptionist: Did you get those tickets from our website?

Darren: Yeah.

Receptionist: Uhhhh… let me check if the movie is being shown here.

Alex and Darren exchange confused looks. The Defenders was the biggest movie that day. How could that place not show the movie?

Receptionist: Sorry, there is no movie named The Defenders.

Darren: What?

Receptionist: I searched the movies that was playing, but The Defenders is not there. I searched the web, but there is no such movie.

Darren: But it's the biggest movie of the year! How on earth has The Defenders movie disappeared?

The receptionist looks at them as if she thought Alex and Darren were out of their minds.

Alex: Thank you for your time! Maybe we got confused. Have a nice day!

Alex grabs Darren's had and starts to walk away.

Darren: No! We have to go back. We paid for those tickets.

Alex: Something is up. I can feel it. Something is not right… Look outside!

The sky was white. Not with white clouds, just white.

Darren: Please tell me that you can see it.

Alex: I can… see, it doesn't come out when I photograph it. We are the only ones who can see it.

Darren: How could we be the only ones?

Alex: This has happened once before, and if anyone on earth would have seen it, there would have been at least one article on it.

Darren: True!

Alex: I have no idea what is happening, and I don't have a good feeling about this. We should go back to X-Cubed.

They rush back to X-Cubed.

Linda: Weren't you going to the movies?

Darren: We were, but we decided, that it was better to… uh…

Alex: Study a little.

Linda: Ok. I don't understand why though. But it's your decision.

Darren: Hey, have you heard of The Defenders?

Linda: Yeah, the heroes who helped us from The V Disaster. Don't you know them?

Alex: We do. We were just asking if you knew them.

Linda: Even an old person knows who The Defenders are… They are world heroes.

Alex and Darren go back to their floor.

Alex: The Defenders are actual people.

Darren: How on earth is that even possible?

Chapter Twelve

THE VISION

Alex's vision turned blurry and everything appeared black. She fell into Darren's arms. Darren takes her to her room. She seemed unconscious, but Alex was actually having a kind of vision. She saw stars-billions of them. She looked around. She was floating in space, but she couldn't see any planets. She felt confused. She then saw the earth. It was translucent, and then she saw another earth, also translucent. There was a white line between them. Then the two earths collided. Alex closed her eyes and braced herself, but when nothing happened. She looked again. It was like the two earths were becoming one. She felt a heavy weight on her shoulders and then she felt herself falling. She was puzzled as she knew that one could not fall in space. Then she realized that she was not in space anymore, she was in a black void. She could hear Darren's voice getting louder.

Darren: Alex! Alex! Hey, are you ok?! Wake up! Should I call Ms Linda?

Alex opens her eyes.

Darren: Oh, my gosh! Alex, are you ok? What happened? Do you need water? Do you need anything?

Alex: I am fine.

Darren: No, you are not. You just fainted. And you weren't waking up.

Alex touches her face. It was all wet.

Alex: Did you put water on my face?

Darren: It was the only thing I could think of.

Alex starts to laugh.

Darren: How are you laughing? I was so worried. I should call Ms Linda.

Alex: No, no, please, I am fine.

Darren: No, you are not.

Alex tries to get up.

Darren: Nope, I am taking you to your room myself.

Alex: What are you talking about? You can't do tha…

Before Alex could finish her sentence, Darren picked her up (seemingly effortlessly), Alex put her hands around his neck for support, and he took her to her room.

Alex remembers what she had seen, and she stops smiling. Darren was at the door.

Alex: Wait Darren… I have to tell you something, please don't call Ms Linda.

Darren sits beside her on the bed.

Darren: What do you want to tell me?

Alex: I had some sort of vision.

Darren: Like a dream?

Alex: Kind of, but it felt real. I think I know why we saw that line. I think I know why everyone disappeared on that plane, and why The Defenders are real. In that vision, I saw earth, and then another earth, and they crashed into each other but not like "crash" crash. It was like they were slowly merging into one earth. Before that, there was a white line between the two earths. It was like they were white earths or white planets, pure white.

Darren: So, you are saying that two earths crashed into each other, and now The Defenders are real?
Alex: No, not two earths. Well yes, but it's so much more than that. When they had passed the white light, it was like the texture of space changed. It was like two dimensions merged into one.
Darren: A parallel dimension?
Alex: I don't know.
Darren: Wait! Are you saying that when two earths' dimensions merged, to cancel out the massive population that would have been created, many people disappeared, and some from the other dimension survived, hence the disappearance of so many people? And as this merge was so silent, no one remembered the disappearance of those people?
Alex: Yes, something like that. Do you think we should tell Linda?
Darren: I don't know.

Chapter Thirteen

THE DEFENDERS

The Defenders are a group of people who have superpowers that they use to fight the enemies of earth. There are five Defenders-Orien, Dale, Landon, Jake and Clio.

Orien

His superpower is that he can read minds. This superpower was thrust upon him, he didn't take it on willingly. He was an assistant in training to a scientist in 1960. The scientist was trying to discover the power of 20% utilization of the brain's capacity. During one of their experiments, the reaction resulted in an explosion of radiation. The scientists were quite far away from the explosion. Orien was the closest to the explosion and went into a deep coma. Several years later, when he woke up, he felt different. Whenever he would look at a person, he could sense the emotion he or she was feeling and a fuzzy reason behind it. When time went on, the fuzzy reasons caused the people's emotions became pictures in Orien's head. He concluded the power he had acquired was the result of the radiation from the explosion. He found that he could strengthen his power by manipulation-not emotional or memory cognition manipulation but he could show people pictures and sometimes visions. He wasn't great at it, but he knew he could do it. Basically, he could create pictures and visions that only a particular person could see.

Dale

Dale is a big computer/math/science genius. He had found a computer in the trash. He took it, examined it, and fixed it. He hadn't parted with it since then. He has immense memory cognition skills. His memory is very powerful. As he grew up, he realized there were memories in his head that weren't his. They were fuzzy memories, but they weren't his. They were his mom's, dad's, and other people he knew. He couldn't use science to find out how he had that power, so he tried to strengthen it over the years.

Landon

Landon's mum was a scientist. She was passionate about what she was doing. She had become pregnant while she was conducting some experiments. The materials she was working with and produced gave off a lot of unknown toxic gas. Unknowingly she had inhaled the gas. She gave birth to Landon, a perfectly healthy baby but she died within a week. Landon was put into foster care. As he grew up, people realized he could run at great speed. He didn't notice it until he saw other kids running.

Jake

Jake's life story was similar to Landon's. Jake lived on a small island. The island had a dormant volcano. However, the volcano erupted when Jake was about five months old. It emitted a lot of radiation. The radiation led to many injuries and fatalities. Jake was the only baby who survived. The survivors raised Jake as their own. People then started to realize that Jake was strong, much stronger than the average child. They knew that if they revealed this to the media, scientists would try to experiment on him. So they kept it a secret.

Clio

Clio grew up with telekinesis. It came to light when she was about six months old. Her parents kept it a secret, but not for long. When Clio turned 22, someone snitched, and she was all over the media. Many scientists invited her to their labs, but she then went into hiding and she was never seen thereafter. Her parents were killed in a car accident a month after she went into hiding. In order to keep a low profile, she got a job as a waiter in a restaurant.

Chapter Fourteen

THE MEETING

It had been a week since Alex had her vision. Since both Darren and Alex witnessed the white light, they thought it was from the merging of the two dimensions. They hadn't told anyone because they knew that if they did, people would start to think of them as weird people. The school board had extended their holiday by another week, though the students didn't know why. On the first day of their extended break, Linda and Ms Larrison Edwards had called in Alex and Darren, early in the morning to the main building. Students rarely go to the main building. Darren and Alex were worried that they were in trouble.

Ms Larrison Edwards: Good morning, students!

Alex and Darren in unison: Good morning, Ms Edwards!

Ms Larrison Edwards: Apologies for calling you in so early, but it was urgent… I can see you are worried. There is no need to be, you are not in trouble. In fact, you are among the best students in this grade. Congratulations!

Alex and Darren look at each other, relief writ large on their faces.

Ms Larrison Edwards: Alex, Timothy Adway had told you about the project he and our team were working on, right?

Alex: Yes.

Ms Larrison Edwards: I'm assuming, Darren, you also know about this?

Darren: The outline of it, yes.

Ms Larrison Edwards: Great! So, I can get straight to the point. Our team detected some activity that occurred eight days ago.

Alex and Darren look at each other. That was the day Alex had had her vision.

Ms Larrison Edwards: But the unusual thing was that we were notified only a day after the sudden activity had happened. So, our team could not identify what it was. Anyway, we have a group of people who want to talk to you about that day.

Alex: Uhhhh, which day?

Ms Larrison Edwards: The day of the plane crash.

Ms Larrison Edwards looks behind them. Alex and Darren turn around to see The Defenders, in the flesh. Alex and Darren experience a roller-coaster of emotions. They are starstruck but at the same time, their heart started to beat faster because they thought they might have caused trouble.

Ms Larrison Edwards: I will leave you.

Ms Larrison Edwards leaves the room.

Landon: Good morning! We apologize for such an early meeting. We were at the Rez Mall the day you were there, and we couldn't help but overhear that you were there for a movie named The Defenders?

Alex and Darren notice Orion looking at them.

Darren: Yeah, we were looking for a movie called The Defenders. Is Dr. Dale looking through my memories?

Dale shakes his head and appears confused.

Orion: How did you know I was rushing through your

memories?

Darren: You were looking at me in a weird manner. I assumed you were doing your thing.

Jake *(in a very deep voice)*: How do you know that he has the power to read a person's memories (mind)?

Alex and Darren become aware of what had happened to them and why they were there.

Darren: Because it was in the movie.

Alex's eyes widen as she looks at Darren. She can't believe he was going to tell them everything and so confidently.

Landon: Movie?

Darren: Yeah.

Alex notices Orien looking at her. She knew that he was trying to read her mind.

Jake: Please elaborate?

Both Darren and Alex start becoming nervous. They don't know how to answer correctly.

Orion: They know a lot about us.

Landon: How can you be sure? Did you?

Orion: Yeah.

Landon: Alex and Darren… right?

Alex and Darren *(in unison)*: Yeah.

Landon: Listen, we talked to Timothy Adway's team. They told us about a sudden shift in our solar system. They also told us about what had happened to you Alex. And we believe you.

Alex looks confused. She didn't want to directly ask them if they believed what happened to her on the airplane.

Alex: What do you believe?

Landon: That you were on the plane, and when you woke up, apparently no one was there. Did that really happen to you?

Alex: Yeah. You believe me?

Jake: To be completely honest, we wouldn't have if a random person told us. But with the data collected, and our experience, what you described is a very likely situation.

Clio: We came here, specifically, because at around 5 pm, something allegedly struck earth. We tracked its location and headed here, but something happened. Whatever that thing was hit the Prosperity building, but when we came here, it was still standing. We tracked it more precisely and saw that it hit the floor where you two were staying. Could you please tell us all the things that happened that day?

Darren: We were planning to go to the movies at around 4 pm. We left X-Cubed at 3.30 pm as we planned to walk to Rez Mall. When the receptionist said that there was no movie called The Defenders, we came back because we felt something was wrong.

Clio: What made you feel that something was wrong?

Darren looks at Alex as she was the one who had felt it all.

Alex: It was just a feeling that something was wrong. We then went outside and saw that the sky was completely white. It wasn't clouds; it was just white. The atmosphere had become dense for a while, but then it returned to normal.

Clio: Why didn't you tell this to anyone?

Darren again looks at Alex. Alex knows what he wants to tell The Defenders about the white line and her vision.

Darren: Because it has happened to us before. It happened the day of the plane crash when Alex's parents allegedly passed away. It happened to Alex but the line was thinner, and then it happened again a week ago. Whenever it happened, we tried to take photos of it, but the camera didn't process the picture.

I asked my friends if they noticed it, but they thought I was making it all up for attention. We knew that no one would believe us, so we never told anyone.

The Defenders exchange glances.

Darren: When we were back in our building, we were just talking about what had happened, and then…

Darren looks at Alex.

Darren: Alex fainted.

Orion: Was it unusual?

Alex: Yeah, I was mentally conscious, I had a vision.

Alex explains what she saw in her vision.

Landon: Guys.

He looks at The Defenders.

Landon: We were right.

Orion: Alex, what you just said proved our theories. Vilch is coming back!

Darren and Alex's eyes widen. Vilch was the Villain of The Defenders. He had come to destroy The Defenders, but when he couldn't, he had said: "I will come back, when two become one, and then three become one. I will destroy the Ring!"

Darren: Vilch? The Skull spear who almost killed you guys?

Landon: How'd you… Wait, right, you know what happened. Yes, he is coming back. When the plane crashed, allegedly, the white sky was, as Alex you saw, two dimensions merging, and then when it happened now, this mix of dimension, merged with the other dimension-two becoming one, then three becoming one. It's happening, he is coming back!

Darren: What is the Ring then?

Landon: We don't really know that. We need to start preparing. Let's go.

Alex and Darren look at each other with terrified and confused looks. They couldn't believe what had just happened, and what was about to happen. Vilch is a very strong force. He can destroy everything. The Defenders were lucky when they won because they could detect Vilch's weakness. But once someone knows their species' (The Skull Spear species) weakness, their weakness changes. And it will be hard to figure out what that weakness is.

Jake: Aren't you guys coming? We don't have all day.

Darren: Wait, you don't mean, we are also going to be fighting Vilch?

Jake: That is what we mean.

Alex: How on earth can two teenagers fight the leader of the Skull Spear Species?

Jake: There is a reason you both remember things from before the merge. You have gone through it twice while remembering things from your original earth. You both have powers, you have to unleash it.

Alex: Powers? We are teenagers! We don't have any powers. We were just lucky or unfortunate to remember things from our original earth.

Jake: You don't understand. The stakes are really high right now. You both have powers. We can feel it and we know when someone has a superpower or not. That thing that we told you about, the thing that hit Prosperity building, the 7th floor, we have visual evidence that it hit you, Alex. It hit you and you fainted. It would have disintegrated any other person. It could have gravely injured us, but it just made you stronger. You now have visions of things that are happening. So, don't say that you don't have powers. You have to come with us. You guys are a very important part of this. Now come.

Darren and Alex look at each other, and then follow Jake and the others.

Uncle Tim: Alex!

Alex: Uncle Tim!

Uncle Tim: Your dad was right about you, you are special.

Alex: What? Are you coming with us?

Uncle Tim: No, honey, I have to stay here. You are going to be ok.

Alex: Please, come with me.

Tears flood Alex's eyes.

Uncle Tim: I have to stay here, honey. You go.

They look at Darren and Jake waiting for them.

Alex: I don't want to leave you. You are the closest thing to family I have.

Uncle Tim: Go, I will always be by your side. You are special, don't ever forget that.

Alex smiles through her tears and then catches up with Darren. They enter a van. Landon tells them that they are taking them to The Defenders' headquarters. Jake gives Alex her backpack. Linda put it there as she knew Alex wouldn't go anywhere without it. Alex held her bag close to herself. Darren could see that Alex was about to burst into tears. He reaches out for her hand and holds it. Alex lays her head on his shoulder. They both eventually fall asleep as they had woken up quite early in the morning.

Chapter Fifteen

HEADQUARTERS

At the headquarters, in a room with multiple hovering screens and a bunch of scientists trying to figure out when the Vilch would be arriving.

Landon: We need to know at least a date for when he is coming.

Orien: Are you being silly?

Alex and Darren were taken slightly aback; it was the first time they had heard Orien speak.

Orien: How would knowing that help us?

Landon: We would be prepared.

Orien: We will never be prepared for the unknown.

Clio: Orien, you have a point, but if there is a way to find out the date, it would help us a little to reduce civilian injuries.

Orien: Right… Should we then just try finding clues from the previous attack?

Landon: Yeah.

Alex leans towards Darren.

Alex: Hey, Darren! Do you remember the first Defenders' movie?

Darren: Yeah.

Alex: Well, when The Defenders were fighting Vilch, he kept waiting to attack. He never purposefully attacked. When one of the Defenders attacked him, only then did he try to put a stone and spear together in the air. Remember?

Darren: Yeah.

Alex: Well, when that happened, the sky went unusually dark. Then Landon ran right next to Vilch, which made him lose his balance. Then the sky became normal again, and Vilch said what he said, and then just left.

Darren: So?

Alex: What if he had to do whatever he needed to do at a specific time? Like during an eclipse?

Darren: That is why he just left after the sky became normal. But wait, didn't the editors say it was a flaw that the screen went dark?

Alex: That is what happened on original earth.

Darren: Ok, but we need more evidence. Let me ask Landon the date of the fight, and then we'll see if anything special happened on that day. Hey, Landon?

Landon: Yeah?

Darren: What was the date of the fight?

Landon: April 27th, 2014. Why?

Darren: Uhh, just curious.

Alex: I found something. The article says that, on April 27th, 2014, the Exi Eclipse occurred. It is a very rare eclipse that happens every six years. It is when the moon appears not equal to or smaller, but bigger that the sun, hence covering the sun as a whole. It lasted for about 10 seconds. It will next happen on the April 27th, 2020… What is today's date?

Darren: April 26th.

Both Alex and Darren in unison: TOMORROW!

Clio: What?

Chapter Sixteen

THE FIRE

Alex and Darren explain their theory to The Defenders. The scientists confirm their research. Vilch was likely to come the next day. Suddenly, Darren's hands start to emit a green light, like a laser. The green light became more focused, and cut an empty chair in half. Darren has unleashed his superpower. Jake gives Darren gloves to prevent him from randomly slicing through things. The glove helped him control his power. There was then a sudden alert announcing that a foreign object had hit a school in Brownstone and started a fire. It was Alex's old school. Alex, Darren and The Defenders take the helicopter to Brownstone. There were at least 10 ambulances and many rescue teams on the site.

Orien: Guys, let's check the meteorite to see if it is likely to explode. Darren and Alex, stay next to an ambulance and help the people. Disperse!

Darren and Alex help those who were unable to walk, to reach the doctors and the ambulances. Alex notices a woman screaming at a fireman.

Lady: Sir, Sir! My DAUGHTER IS NOT HERE!

Fire man: She must be at the rescue centre for the kids, Ma'am, go check there.

Lady: SHE IS NOT THERE! SHE IS STILL IN THE BUILDING!

Firemen: Ma'am, everyone has been escorted out of the building. There is no one in the building.

Lady: YOU HAVE TO UNDERSTAND, SHE IS IN THERE!

Fire Men: Lady, can you please move? There are injured people here, I am trying to save their lives. Please, visit the child rescue centre.

Alex walks over to the lady.

Alex: Ma'am, what is the problem?

Lady: My daughter is still in the building, on the ground floor, in the bathroom in the right wing. I know she is there. She told me she was in the bathroom before this damn rock fell on us.

Alex: I will notify the other firemen, and we will rescue your daughter.

Alex makes her way to Darren and tells him about it. But he says that if the firemen had got everyone out, it is likely the girl is out too. Alex has a gut feeling that the woman's daughter is still in the building. She goes towards the building. The fire was getting stronger. She finds a spare fire-resistant jacket and quickly puts it on. She then goes to the backdoor that was connected to the girl's bathroom in the right wing. Having attended the school for so many years, Alex knew every corner of the building.

Darren: Alex, there is a teenage boy there. Bring him… Alex?

Darren looks around for Alex but can't find her.

Darren: Alex, Alex!

Alex goes to the backdoor, opens it and sees that the flames were going towards the bathroom stalls. She saw a girl, next to the mirrors, unconscious. Alex picks her up and hurries out. She then tries to make her way out, but she realizes that she is trapped. She sees a small narrow space and runs through that, trying her hardest to protect the child. She makes her way to an ambulance and hands the child to the doctors. Alex finds it difficult to breathe properly and makes her way to Darren. Almost all the people were at the rescue centres, and Darren was almost done.

Darren: Alex! Oh my gosh! Where the heck were you? Did you go into the building?

Alex: There was a girl in there. She could have died. The firemen didn't listen, and you didn't listen either.

The child's mother approaches Alex.

Lady: Thank you for saving my daughter! How can I ever repay you? I am so grateful for what you did.

Alex: I only did what I needed to do.

Alex started to choke and her vision becomes blurry.

Alex: Darren…

Alex falls into Darren's arms.

Darren: Alex! Alex!

Chapter Seventeen

KARA

Alex had inhaled some of the toxic fumes from the fire. That is why she couldn't breathe and became unconscious. She woke up in the hospital.

Darren: Alex! Hey!

Alex: Hey, Darren!

Alex holds tightly to Darren's hand.

Darren: Don't ever do that again!

Alex: Save someone when no one else would?

Darren: Sorry.

Alex: It's ok.

Alex smiles.

Landon: You feeling better?

Alex: I'm feeling great.

Landon: You need to rest for the night. We have a big day tomorrow, but you are not going to be out there.

Alex: Why?

Landon: You don't have your powers yet.

Alex: I can still help.

Landon: No, you can't risk it, and that is settled.

Orien enters the room.

Orien: Hey, could I talk to Alex, alone?

Everyone leaves the room.

Orien: That was foolish!

Alex: Why?

Orien: You could have died.

Alex: I didn't have a choice. No one believed me. I had to help the girl.

Orien: What if there was no girl?

Alex: I knew that there was a girl in there. Anyway, why do you care?

Orien: Kara cared.

Alex's eyes widened. She hadn't told anyone except Darren about Kara.

Alex: How do you know Kara?

Orien: It's time you know.

Alex: Know what?

Orien: Do you remember the story of the radiation explosion?

Alex: The one that sent you into a coma?

Orien: Well, before that, I had a significant other named Kara. She told me a lot about the universe but also left a lot of questions unanswered. The last thing she ever spoke to me before she died was that the next time I would see her, it would be as a teenager in the future. She told me that she wouldn't talk to me when I saw her, but I'd know that it was her. She also told me that I should take care of a girl called Alex as she is special and would be the next…

Alex: The next?

Orien: She couldn't finish. I went into coma, and when I woke up, I tried to find Kara. When I did, I saw her with you in Brownstone. She looked at me and I knew. It was Kara. I then left and never went back. When we first called you up at the main building at X-Cubed, I knew it was you the minute I saw you. Kara was right, you are special. I couldn't read your mind. Dale told me when he was trying to examine your memory and Darren's but he couldn't. That is saying a lot because both of us can access any person/creature's mind. We went through Vilch's mind, but we couldn't get through to yours. Alex, you are special.

Alex: Wait, so, you are saying that you knew Kara?

Orien: Yeah.

Alex: Do you know her favorite animal?

Both Alex and Orien: Chameleon.

Orien: She liked chameleons a lot. She loved when the chameleon changed colour on a tree, never on grass.

Alex was shocked.

Orien: Sorry I called you foolish. I didn't want you to die. You still have a big purpose to fulfill in this universe. Serve that purpose.

Landon barges in the room.

Landon: The meteorite had an exact element match to Vilch's army boat!

Chapter Eighteen

VILCH'S ARRIVAL

The next day, the day of Vilch's arrival. Alex wakes up in the hotel where everyone had taken shelter. She looked outside. She saw the sun rising and then, suddenly, everything around her disappeared. She could see herself, but nothing around her. She hears something behind her and turns around to see Vilch running towards her. She braced herself, but Vilch went right through her. She realized that Vilch was running away from something and she adjusted her eyes. She saw some type of golden light. It was the size of her fingers. The golden light turned into circular rings. They surround Vilch and he explodes. Her surroundings become clear. She is back in the real world. She is startled by the sound of an alarm. Darren enters her room.

Darren: It's here.

They make their way to the headquarters.

Scientist 1: Something unknown has entered the earth's atmosphere and is coming right at us. EVACUATE!!!!

Everyone evacuates the building. Clio and Alex get the weapons and run out of the building.

Alex: Where is Dale?

Clio: He is at another site, activating our weapons.

They see huge ships coming towards a building and crash into it. The building shatters. One piece flies towards Alex. Darren pushes Alex behind a car, and then using his power, cuts the building in half.

Vilch: Well, well, well… who do we have here? The Defenders! Who can't even defend a school.

Jake: Says the guy who lost last time.

Vilch: QUIET!

Orien: He is about to bring out the army.

Landon rushes towards Vilch but is pushed back by some kind of force field. Just as Landon hits the ground, monsters in the shape of snakes come out of the spaceships. Suddenly everyone starts to run. Everyone uses their weapons and powers to kill the monsters. Alex stays behind Darren, but he was jumping from one car to another. Alex decided to hide behind a car. A monster charges at her, but stops in mid-air, and then crumples to dust. Her eyes widen. She stands up to see if it was Clio who had helped her, but sees no one. Alex then goes into the nearest building. She hides behind the receptionist's table. She suddenly hears the doors open and then clash and shatter into pieces. She was hoping it was Darren who had just killed a monster. But it was the monster. She saw it look under the table to see if anyone was there. Alex looked away and put her hands up as some kind of protection against the monster. From the corner of her eye, she sees the monster open its mouth, but no sound comes out. She saw the same circular rings that she had seen in the dream she had in the morning coming from her hands. She used her hands and the circular force/heat fields to slam the monster against the wall. She looks at her hands in shock, and then sees it turn gold in colour. She realises she was the golden light and that she had to kill Vilch. She went out of the building.

She sees the moon starting to cover the sun. She saw Vilch hold up his spear. It was time. The spear's power hit everyone-Jake, Darren, Clio, Landon and Orien. Alex runs toward Vilch, she realises that she was above the ground, she was flying. She sees Landon trying to charge at Vilch.

Alex: STAY BACK!

Landon sees Alex with her golden rings. He obeyed. Alex flies over Vilch and surrounds him with rings. The closer she is, the more Vilch loses his power.

Clio: Is that-

Darren: Alex!

Landon: Guys, the moon has covered the sun.

Vilch explodes into thin air. The monsters start to explode similarly into thin air. Alex falls down, unconscious.

Chapter Nineteen

LETTING GO

A week later. In the hospital.

Darren: Hey! How are you feeling?

Alex: Better.

Darren: That really drained all your energy out, didn't it?

Alex: It did.

Darren: We are all over the media. Jade and Jaden wanted to call and see you. When would you be able to do it?

Alex: Maybe sometime in the evening?

Darren: Ok, I'll text them.

Orien enters the room. He wears a serious expression.

Orien: Alex, your uncle is in a coma.

Alex: What?

Orien: He fell into a coma unexpectedly. The doctors are trying to find a cause but have had no success as yet. He is still breathing, but we don't know when he will wake up.

Alex is speechless. Thing go dark around her. She can see herself, but not her surroundings. She looks around and sees Uncle Tim. She runs to him.

In Alex's vision.

Alex: What happened to you?!

Uncle Tim: What was meant to be. Listen, there is a very big chance that I will not wake up from this coma.

Alex: Don't say that!

Alex starts to tear up.

Uncle Tim: Don't cry, I will be joining Robert, Helene, Tom, Jenna and Kara.

Alex: Where?

Uncle Tim: You won't understand where, but we are always looking upon you.

Tim stands aside and Alex sees her mom, dad, Kara and Kara's parents. She tries to run to them, but they keep going farther away from her.

Uncle Tim: You can't reach them. Listen to me. Robert, Helene, Tom, Jenna and Kara were heroes in another dimension a long, long time ago. We are here to pass it on. We have chosen and finished our purpose in the universe. Now it's your turn. Fulfill your purpose.

Alex *(sobbing)*: So, I will not get to see you again?

Uncle Tim: Not for the time being. But always remember…

Alex: You are always looking upon me.

Uncle Tim: Goodbye, honey. You are a light, fulfill your purpose.

Alex comes back to reality. Darren is beside her.

Darren: Hey, how are you feeling? You cried in your sleep.

Alex: Uncle Tim isn't coming back.

Darren: Don't say that. There is still hope.

Alex: No, he is gone. Now it's time to fulfill our purpose in the universe.

Darren: I really don't understand what you are saying.

Alex: It's complicated. Could you please get me some coffee? I haven't had one in days.

Darren: There she is!

Darren and Alex still go to X-Cubed. Along with that, they are training to be an official part of the Defenders. Alex and Darren had a small party after everything was over.

Darren: I am so glad it's all over!

Alex: Me too!

OR WAS IT?

REAL INTELLIGENCE

Chapter 1

NEW STUDENT

Student 1: There is a transfer student.

Student 2: Really? We've never actually had one.

Student1: Her name is Ryan.

Mr Brown: Good morning class. Today, we have a new transfer, her name is Ryan.

Class (*in unison)*: Welcome!

Mr Brown: Ryan, you can go and sit down next to Sam.

Ryan goes towards the boy Mr Brown pointed to. She puts her bag down, trying to focus on the desk, but she is unable to because of her new surroundings. The class that she had just entered was nothing like she had ever seen. She sat down and regained her focus. She realised that she had sat down next to someone and hadn't bothered to say anything. Before she could say anything, Sam smiled at her.

Sam: Hey! Ryan Right?

Ryan brings herself to talk.

Ryan: Yeah, hi! Nice to meet you.

Sam: Nice to meet you too.

Mr Brown: Ok class, open up your tablets and please log into your accounts to start our session.

Ryan starts to look for a tablet. She sees the other students take out their shiny, polished, mirror-like tablets out of a clear case and set it on their desks. Sounds of typing and clicking of buttons can be heard. Ryan begins to panic as she looks down at her worn-out brown leather bag and realizes that the only things she has in her bag are a few notebooks and a pencil case. She looks towards Mr Brown, hoping that he would look at her and realise that she does not have a tablet. She dreaded having to stand up and ask him herself. To Ryan's relief, Mr Brown does notice her situation.

Mr Brown: Ah, Ryan, I have your tablet. Could you please come and collect it?

Ryan walks up to the front of the class, trying not to make eye contact with the few students who had turned their heads towards her.

Mr Brown: Here is your tablet, and here is your username and password for your account. If you have any trouble, feel free to ask.

Ryan looks at the paper with her username and password, and then looks at the tablet. Excitement runs through her veins. She hurries back to her desk, and opens her case. She handles them carefully as she sets the tablet down.

Sam: Not trying to be rude, but you don't really have to be that careful with the tablet. They are quite strong. The top layer of the tablet is made of a Gorilla Glass 6 protector, and the case is durable and is meant to protect the tablet from any sort of hock due to a drop or fall.

Ryan: Oh, ok. I'm very new to this, and it's fascinating holding a tablet.

Sam: New? Didn't you have tablets when you did home schooling?

Ryan: Home school?

Sam: Yeah, home school. Most students come to Mega Tech because it is the only tech school, but some students home school until high school starts. Weren't you home schooled before? I have not seen you around in Middle school.

Ryan: Oh! I didn't know that I actually am from The Bracket.

Sam: Oh, I didn't know that, not many people join schools like this from The Bracket.

Ryan: Yeah, I'm actually the first from my community. I wanted to see what this place is like.

Sam: So, are you enjoying it so far?

Ryan: Extremely!

Chapter 2

WORLD WAR III

Ryan looks at the tablet, trying to understand how to work it. She touches the edge of the tablet, she presses the button she found there, but nothing happened.

Sam: Can I help?

Ryan: Please!

Sam smiles and explains how the tablet works. She picked up the information quite quickly, and like the rest of the class, they both do their math assignments. Ryan was used to doing things on a piece of paper and was a bit slow in answering the questions on the assignment. She was, however, quite a bright student. She loved to learn. She loved everything, from biology to complex mathematics. She finished her assignments a little slower than she would have if she had done it on paper. Once the assignments were done, her eyes gleamed and twinkled as the screen changed to a different tab. A feeling of excitement washed over her. Ryan had always wanted to go to this school-Mega Tech. Technology fascinated her. She came from a community called The Bracket. The other community was called The Sustainers. (The communities within The Bracket were quite strict. Her community was the same nonetheless). On the contrary The Sustainers had its foundation in technology, while still trying to sustain the environment. Ryan's community, like the others, was strictly against technology. The members believed that technology made people carefree and lazy. Telephone was the only technological instrument that communities in The Bracket used. Although Ryan did agree that technology made people lazier, she could see the potential of technology and how its advancement could benefit the earth and the people. She knew how it can reveal the secrets of the universe. She was able to see a 'twin' of the world, where people used technology the right way, advancing to new heights, while still preserving its natural beauty. Unfortunately, the 'twin' was only a dream. The reason why The Bracket people did not like technology and wanted to have nothing to do it dates back to a time when technology was at its peak. Ryan's planet was rapidly inventing new technology every year, almost every month. Everyone enjoyed the luxuries that technology provided. Most human beings took advantage of it, and misused technology. They took technology and its luxuries for granted. People became lazier and lazier, while technology advanced. People lost the motivation to do common day jobs because technology took care of that. The environment suffered immensely, yet most of mankind didn't give it a thought. Not a single thought! Just like an organ starts to fail when the body suffers, the planet started to fail. Countries started to become unhabitable either due to extreme temperatures from climate change or due to the huge amounts of pollution on land, in the water, and in air. The planet had become a plastic planet. This is around the time that Ryan was born. She was born when the planet's most intelligent species went from 8 billion to 2 billion, which happened either due to the extreme weather changes or the World War. This was the Third War that had occurred, but this war was not between countries. It was between people of different interests. The whole world was divided into two sections-the people who wanted technology to stop and who opposed it completely and those who could see the benefits. There were a few who could look at what the positive side of technology could achieve. The war ended with a huge number of fatalities, resulting in more than half the population dying. Ryan can barely remember her parents. She grew up in a care-center, better known as a community within The Bracket. Her community, like others, helped children who had lost their parents in the war. Ryan was one of them. As a child, she was told that her parents had gone somewhere, but they did not know when they would to come back. Ryan knew more. At the age of about 5, she had found a letter under her bed. It was not exactly a letter, it was a screened tablet of some sort. Even at the age of 5, she knew that technology was not accepted in her community, so she kept that tablet hidden. The tablet consisted of a video letter from her parent, telling her that they had to go to the war, and that they would come back. The war ended when Ryan was four. She didn't understand much of what her parents had said in that video letter, but as she grew up and understood things more, she realised that her parents may have not survived. The community Ryan lived with was called The Carreens. The Carreens were a relaxed community compared to the others. They had told the children living there about the war, and why it had occurred. They also did not loudly express their hatred of technology, but one could deduce that the elders who ran the community did not necessarily side with technology. When Ryan turned 12, she and her peers were introduced to many high schools, including a school called Mega Tech. It was the only school run by The Sustainers. The children, from the age of 12 had to start thinking of their choice of high school because they would accordingly learn the necessary things required by the school. Every child chose to go, or was prepared to go to a high school that was situated within The Bracket. People from Mega Tech would come to the 12-year old's and tell them about the school and how it worked. Although many children were fascinated and did have Mega Tech as one of their high school choices, their choice and opinion about the school changed over time due to their parents and elders in The Bracket community. They told the children how horrible Mega Tech was or how bad technology was. And why it was the cause of World War III. Listening to all this, the children would be reluctant to have Mega Tech as their high school of choice. Ryan, despite these stories, was determined to go to Mega Tech. She had made a scrapbook of things she wanted to do if she was able to go to Mega Tech. Ryan's best friend Blaire was also fascinated by technology, but she was conflicted. Her parents, and many she knew told her about the dangers of technology . Ryan could only do so much to convince her. Ryan on the other hand, wanted to prove to the others that technology can be used for the betterment of planet, if only people use it the right way. Ryan signed up for the Mega Tech Programme. Although she couldn't prepare for it, because she did not have the resources, she tried her best to excel in what she was doing. She was 15 when they went to high school. On the day of their Middle School graduation, Ryan was accepted by Mega Tech. She was the only one from The Bracket to be chosen for Mega Tech. Blaire, in the end let her parents' and elders' judgement get the better of her and chose a high school within The Bracket. When Ryan was being presented with her certificate, no one clapped for her, and all the teachers and parents gave her uncomfortable glances. The only people that applauded her for her achievement was her Carreens counselor-Ms Jane, and her closest friend-Blaire. The people who presented her with the award rigorously washed their hands afterwards because, a Mega Tech certificate is given on a tablet. Present day. Ryan was welcomed by The Sustainers, she was shown around the school, and was told all the things that would be done. As, for her it was like entering a whole new world. The moment she stepped foot in the precinct of the Sustainers, she knew, that this was a new chapter in her life that she was ready to face head on. Back in the classroom.

Mr Brown: Time is up!

The students groan because they weren't able to finish the assignment.

Mr Brown: I didn't intend for you guys to finish the assignment in one class. We will continue this in our next class.

Everyone let out a sigh of relief.

Mr Brown: Class dismissed, have a nice day! Ryan, could you please stay for five minutes after class if you don't mind?

Ryan: Of course, sir.

Ryan packs everything, and approaches Mr Brown. Her heart starts to beat faster as she approaches the table.

Mr Brown: I just checked my class list, and it says you have finished your assignment.

Ryan: Oh, yeah, I finished mine. I didn't know I was not supposed to.

Mr Brown: Oh, no, it is completely fine that you finished it. It is actually surprising that you did. I understand that you came from The Bracket, right?

Ryan: Yes.

Mr Brown: Well, what they had taught you there has clearly benefited you, and I think you will do very well in our Extended Programme for Mathematics!

Ryan: Really? Wow, that would be great! I thought you were going to send me back to The Bracket. Oh, what a relief!

Mr Brown: Why would you think such a thing? It is an honour to have a student from The Bracket join Mega Tech. As you may have seen, you are the only one from The Bracket and you may think that we, The Sustainers, have some sort of dislike for The Bracket, but it is the opposite. We respect and understand the views of The Bracket and hope that at some future point in time, technology would be given a better role.

Ryan: I did not know that.

Mr Brown: Well, it is how it is. Anyway, you better get along to your next class.

Ryan: Thank you, sir! Have a nice day!

Mr Brown: You too!

Chapter 3

NEW EXPERIENCES

Ryan exits the classroom, her heart beating with joy. She could do the Extended Programme! This news was the right thing to calm her nerves. She went to all of her classes that day, and learnt far too many things to process in a day. After her last class, the receptionist she had met at the beginning of the day, took her to her dormitory building. The building was tall and narrow with huge glass windows that seemed as if they were tinted black. They entered the building, and everything inside was so different from what Ryan had imagined. The receptionist glances at Ryan and notices her expression.

Receptionist: I know this probably looks like a hotel, but trust me, the 1st floor is when this building starts to look like a dormitory.

Ryan: This… this is what hotels look like? Wow!

Receptionist: Yeah, they do. Come on, let's go to the fifth floor, we'll get you your dorm card.

The step into the elevator. Ryan is stunned by everything around her – the white shiny tables, the immense number of computers on the ground floor, the glass elevator. It was nothing like anything she had seen before.

Ryan: Hey, I didn't get your name.

Receptionist: Pardon me, my name is Olivia.

Ryan: So, Ms Olivia, can you please tell me more about this place? The dormitory because it is completely different from the Bracket, so I'm assuming the rules here are different too?

Olivia: Firstly, call me Olivia-no need for such formalities. I am a senior in high school. So, I'm like a friend.

Ryan: Senior in high school? Then how are you the receptionist as well?

The elevator stops on the 6th floor. The doors open into a more relaxed room. The walls were painted a cream color. There were at least two big sofas, a glass coffee table books and a soft carpet on the floor. Ryan felt a little close to home here.

Olivia: As a senior, we have to get internships at any job where you can learn management skills, so I offered to become the receptionist and help welcome new students to school. Let's get you your card, then I'll tell you more about this building.

They went up to the lady at the desk that said Receptionist, and picked up five very shiny dorm cards.

Ryan: Why five cards?

Olivia: Well, many students lose theirs and it is a long process to get another one. So we have started to hand out five, so at least they have backups.

They enter the elevator and start going up. Ryan could see the city from there. She deduced that her floor was quite high up.

Olivia: This is the girls dormitory building. Up to the 5th floor are rooms for all the female teachers, and then the 5th floor to the 15th floor are rooms for the students.

Ryan: The 15th floor?

Olivia: Yeah, it is a pretty big building. The teachers aren't allowed to go to floors above the 5th, and students aren't allowed to go to floors 1-5, just to maintain space, and to avoid any major interactions so that this experience allows the student to feel like they are home.

The elevator bell dings and Ryan follows Olivia through a corridor with doors to the left and right. The corridor was narrow, but wasn't as high-tech as the rest of the building. There was a fluffy red carpet on the ground. The walls were painted cream and the lights were a golden color. Olivia stopped next to a door with the number 158. She opens a sort of mailbox attached next to the door on the wall and swipes the card against the black glass. The white door automatically opens into a small dorm room. It had a small but tall white desk with lights, a small but comfortable bed, two cabinets adjacent to the door and a large window.

Olivia: This is your dorm room. Here are your cabinets. Your suitcases are over there (*pointing towards the three suitcases next to the bed).* Next to your desk, there is a packet, which has all the other things you will need. You can organize them yourself and the bed. Underneath the bed are organizational drawers if you require more space for storage. The bathroom is at the end of this corridor. It is a communal bathroom, but the bathroom is divided so that there is a small cubicle for each member on this floor. Yours will be Cab 158, same number as your dorm. If you have any problems, you can call the number on the dorm website.

Ryan: The dorm website?

Olivia: I almost forgot. Have you been given your tablet and your account?

Ryan: Yeah, I got it first thing in the morning.

Olivia: Great, then, in a moment, you will receive an email giving you the steps to access various websites that you will need to know about. The phone number on that website would be the one you call for any help.

The lady behind the counter: Oh ok, thank you!

Olivia: Well, have a great rest of the day!

Olivia exits the dorm room, and moments later, Ryan hears a ringing shattering the silence and startling her. She went up to the door, saw a black screen similar to the one outside. She looked around for the cards she was given, and then swiped them one by one. To Ryan's relief, the door opened and she saw Olivia standing there.

Olivia: I am so sorry. I'm never usually this forgetful. I haven't told you about your breakfast, lunch and dinner and where you can have food! Come with me, I'll show you the cafeteria.

Olivia takes her to the 6th floor where they meet the same receptionist again. The corridor that Olivia was taking Ryan through, was much more spaced out and a little less cozy as the lights were white. There was no carpet, the walls were alternating between a light grey color and white. They walk to the end of the short corridor and approach a big pair of doors. Olivia takes a card out of her pocket, a different card, swipes it against the same black glass on the door, which opens into a huge cafeteria. The cafeteria had many tables across the room, and towards the right, she saw a buffet with food and drinks. Ryan couldn't imagine how such a big room could fit in here.

Olivia: This is the cafeteria.

Ryan: It's… it's so big!

Olivia: Yeah, many people who first come in here have the same views. But people underestimate the dimensions of this building. So, you could come here any time you would like, from 5 am till around 11pm.

Ryan: Such long hours! How so? Where is the food made?

Olivia: The food is made in the kitchen, that connects the two buildings.

Ryan: The two buildings?

Olivia: We came in through Door Exit 3, you couldn't have seen it. This building is part of a three-part complex. There are two buildings-one with the female dormitories and the other for the male dormitories. The third building connects the two buildings, and that is the kitchen – where all the food is made.

Ryan: That must require a lot of work! Making food for so many people. How do you even get the resources?

Olivia: We use technology and the research to help sustain the planet. At least in our region of the planet, we have found a lot of ways to obtain resources without damaging it. Our region has a huge eco-garden in the centre, and almost everyone who lives in this region volunteers to run that farm. Everyone here contributes everywhere. Plus there aren't a lot of people in the Sustainers-5000 is our population.

Ryan: 5000? I thought there were 500 million people in The Sustainers.

Olivia: Well, yes, there are, but we are spread out across the world as headquarters of the Sustainers. This region that we are staying in, is the T quarter, where children come to learn and teachers and some people with jobs here, live. That is why there are only 5000 people.

Ryan: Oh, I get it, I didn't know that.

Olivia: How would you? I don't think The Bracket talks about The Sustainers in that way.

Ryan: Yeah, that is true-but I have one more question. If the children want to study here, then how is it that there are so few children in school?

Olivia: Well, Mega Tech is the only school that still goes to the Bracket to advertise their school. Other schools..

Ryan: Other Schools?

Olivia: Yeah, other schools stopped advertising their schools to the Bracket because, no one joined.

Ryan: Oh!

Olivia: Oh, and I almost forgot, you can find all sorts of things on your floor as well-like a gym and a study space. We turned right when we got to the 10th floor, well if you go to your left, you will find doors which say 'gym' and "study space." Your card will work on those doors. I think that is about it. You can go to your dorm room now, and if you want to call family and friends, just know that you can make five calls from your tablet each day. This is done so that we don't use much power-you know to...

Ryan: Sustain the earth? Yeah, I figured. Thank you so much for clearing things up for me. It was really helpful. Have a nice day!

Olivia: No worries!

Chapter 4

HOME SICK

Ryan leaves the cafeteria and walks across the corridor, looking for the elevator. She went up to her dorm and sat on her bed, looking out her window. She could barely see the other building, but the view was amazing. She saw a building that looked like a circular stadium where the eco-gardens were. She remembered that she had to call Ms Jane and Blaire. She took her tablet and tries to figure out how to call someone. She found an icon that looked like a phone, and tapped it. She typed Jane's number on the keypad and called.

Ryan: Hello?

Ms Jane: Please direct me to Mega Tech Academy, Ryan Sierra…

Ryan: Hi, Ms Jane! It's me, Ryan.

Ms Jane: That was fast.

Ryan: You didn't have to direct the phone call. If you call this number, the call will come to me directly.

Ms Jane: Oh! That is great! How was your first day?

Ryan: I don't know where to start. This place is so different. We had all our classes on tablets and we had to submit our work on the them too. In mathematics, I was asked to join the Extended Programme because I did really good on an assignment. They strictly forbid plastic bottles, just like in The Bracket, even the reusable ones.

Ms Jane: Wow! I am so proud of you. I am sure you must have gone to the library during your break, didn't you?

Ryan: No. Well, sort of. They don't really have a library.

Ms Jane: That's terrible.

Ryan: But they have something called an e-library where you can access books on your tablet itself. It isn't like a real library, and it doesn't feel the same as reading an actual book, but they said that it is done so that people don't have to waste paper and cut many trees to produce books. So, they are trying to save the environment.

Ms Jane: Wow! That's an interesting way of saving the environment.

Ryan: Yeah! They have so many rules here that are majorly meant to save the environment. Enough about me. How are you doing?

Ms Jane: I am alright.

Ryan: How are The Carreens?

Ms Jane: Nothing has changed, the same routine, same people, same drama. Many people are still talking about how you left to study at Mega Tech, but the curiosity is dying out.

Ryan hears an unusual sound – the sound of a bell ringing.

Ryan: What was that?

Ms Jane: It is time for me to go. Do call me whenever you are free. Be safe!

Ryan: Bye M…

The phone gets disconnected. Ryan calls Blaire, hoping that it would be she who picks up the phone because in a place like The Carreens, even the telephone booth is communal.

Ryan: Hello?
Blaire: Can you please direct me to Mega Tech, Ryan Sie-
Ryan: Blaire! It's me, Ryan.
Blaire: Ryan? Hi! Oh my Gosh! That was fast.
Ryan: Ms Jane said that too. If you call this number, you will be calling me directly.
Blaire: Really? Wow!

Ryan and Blaire talked for around 15 minutes. Blaire says that people were starting to give her disapproving looks. So they ended the call. Ryan put down her tablet and looked out the window. She felt homesick. Even though she had been waiting for this day for a long time, she missed The Carreens-especially Ms Jane and Blaire. Memories of her days at The Carreens came flooding back. She remembered how they went to the park and played. She remembered the stacks of books in the library. She remembered the sleepovers with Blaire. Ryan shook her head and said to herself, "You have always wanted to be here. Blaire and Ms Jane will always be there to call. Pull yourself together." She stood up and started to unpack her suitcase. She organized her room and her desk. She found buttons all over the room. One button activated the window slider, a white cover that covered the window like a curtain. Another button opened the cabinets and yet another revealed a television and a television box with a remote. Ryan's heart leaped with joy because she had never seen or touched a television. She had only seen it in the few books she read on technology. By the time she finished exploring and organizing her room, it was dinner time. She went to the cafeteria but there was no one there except for the ladies who worked there.

Ryan: Hello!

The lady behind the counter: Hello! You must be Ryan.
Ryan: Yeah. How did you know?
The lady behind the counter: Well, all the staff were told about you. You are the first to come from The Bracket. Hi! I am Amelia.
Ryan: Hi! I was just wondering, where everyone was. I thought that it was dinner time.
Amelia: It is indeed, but dinners are always done with both the girls and the boys. This time, the boys will be coming over to this side.
Ryan: Oh! I thought that this was the girls' dormitory.
Amelia: Well, it is, but, as we want the students to bond and become a well-knit family, dinners are done together. They come through the hallway that connects Building 1 (this one) and Building 3 (the boy's dormitory). Weren't you told about this?
Ryan: I think they may have forgotten to tell me.
Amelia: Well, they will be coming in around 15 minutes. Would you like to start your dinner?
Ryan: Yes, please! I am famished.

Amelia explained how Ryan could choose her dinner. Ryan took the foods that she was most familiar with-beans with rice and lentil soup. The other dishes were not known to her. She chose a table in the corner of the cafeteria, took out her tablet and started to eat while reading a book. She had finished dinner and was starting to head out when she heard loud chatter. The cafeteria doors opened and the students filed in. Soon the cafeteria was full. Many of the students glanced at Ryan. She tried not to look conscious and continued to read. She found a place to dispose her plate and slipped out. She felt overwhelmed since she didn't really know anyone there, except for the few people she had briefly talked to in class. She hurried back to her dorm room, and sat at her desk. She had tasks to finish.

Chapter 5

THE COMPETITION

It had been around four months since Ryan came to Mega Tech. It had been hard for her to adjust and adapt to the new lifestyle, but she eventually did, and was now living the dream she had been wanting for a long time. She had made a few friends in Mega Tech. She wasn't as close to them as she was with Blaire because most of them had known each other since they were kids. She found her whole grade to be friendly and nice. It was a surprise to her. She had heard that people from The Sustainers weren't usually nice. But The Bracket was probably biased. In those four months, they had done a lot. Ryan was offered the Extended Programme in mathematics and physics. She had been working really hard for the semester finals. All the exams were done on computers and tablets. The final exam challenged knowledge and teamwork. The grade was divided into six groups. Each group had five persons. And the group had to compete against each other in a quiz in mathematics, physics, history and sustainability. The catch was that you weren't told who'd be in your group until the final day of the semester finals, the day of the quiz. Ryan worked hard for this and finally the day arrived. Ryan was at her desk. She looked at the time. It was 7.55 am. She had five minutes before she had to go for breakfast, and then to school for the quiz. She quickly skimmed through all the tables open on her laptop, trying to cover as much as she could. She hurried to the cafeteria, met Kate and Birdie (two friends she had made), ate her breakfast, and along with her friends, went to school for the last final exam-the quiz. They arrived at the examination hall just in time. The hall was completely different compared to the day before. All the computer desks and desk dividers were gone. Instead there were six big desks spread out around the room with buzzer buttons on them and a huge scoreboard hung from the ceiling. The students crowded near the main door, facing the scoreboard. The examiners stood on a podium beneath the scoreboard.

The examiner in the middle: Welcome, students! I am Mrs Mia, one of your examiners today. Welcome to your last final-The Quiz. Your teams will be displayed on the scoreboard above in a moment. Here are the rules. When your team has been identified, you will quietly go to your selected tables, and discuss any strategies in the given three minutes. Then the quiz will begin. The examiners will ask the questions, and additionally the question will be displayed on the screen above. You will have around 20 seconds to discuss, and the first team to press the buzzer, answers. The buzzer can also be pressed within the 20 seconds given. If the wrong answer is given, no points will be deducted, and the second fastest team that pressed the buzzer will answer. No one should shout out the answer. Please respect the other teams. And if you call out the answer, you will get a warning, and if you continue, you will be disqualified and will have to write two alternative examinations. As the teams were pre-decided, they cannot be changed, and there are three students who will not be able to make it and will take the alternate two examinations. Unfortunately, the three students are from the same team. Although this may seem unfair, we are not able to change it. Hence, if the students in that team perform average or above average, he or she will be given bonus points. (Students groan.) The teams will be displayed now.

Ryan looks for her name frantically, and finds she is in the team with only two players. Nervousness courses through her veins. She looks at the other name, Will. She had met Will in her classes and had talked to him, but not much. She knew that he was a member of many of the clubs, especially the sports and the music clubs. She realized that most of the students had already gone to their tables. She rushes to her table, where Will is already standing.

Mrs Mia: Your three minutes begin now.

The scoreboard screen changes to a ticking clock, counting down.

Will: Hey, Ryan, right?

Ryan: Yeah!

Will: So… this is our team.

Ryan: Yeah… I really don't know what to say.

Will: Me neither.

Both laugh.

Will: Ok, but we really need to strategize.

Ryan: What do you specialize in? Like which are your strongest subjects?

Will: History and physics.

Ryan: Ok, mine is mathematics and physics.

Will: Sustainability can be dealt with by both of us.

Ryan: Ok, so, let's agree that for history, you will answer, for math I will. And for sustainability and physics, we'll work as a team.

Will: Works for me, but when a question comes and one of us is not certain, we should discuss as fast as we can.

Ryan: Agreed.

Mrs Mia: Time is up. Students, get ready. This is your first question.

The first few questions were quite hard for Ryan and Will, especially because they were not able to come up with the answers fast enough. But by half-time, they re-thought their strategy, and quickly climbed up the leaderboard and won.

Mrs Mia: And the winners are… Will and Ryan!

The room reverberated with applause, and everyone was looking at Will and Ryan.

Will: We did it!

Ryan: We did!

Will and Ryan hurried towards the examiners for their medal and certificate.

Mrs Mia: We didn't think you would be able to do it, but you guys fought and came up tops. Congratulations! Well done!

Both Will and Ryan: Thank you!

Will and Ryan go back to their table when the next award was announced.

Will: Wow! We did it!

Ryan: Yeah, we did! I wasn't sure we would be able to though.

Will: Had the same feeling! We make a good team! At least for people who don't know each other, right?

Ryan: Yeah.

Mrs Mia: So, this is the end of your finals. (*Turning to all the students*) Dinner will begin soon. Today it will be in Building 3. Girls, you have to be there in a maximum of 30 minutes.

All the girls hurry back to their dorms. Ryan places her medal on her desk and heads down for dinner. She approaches the door which leads to Building 3, but no one is there. She first thought that maybe everyone had already eaten and left, but it wasn't possible. She had just seen a group of girls on her floor hurry to the bathroom. She looked around and sees Will approaching her.

Will: Hey!

Ryan: Hi!

Will: Aren't you up with the girls? Like getting ready?

Ryan: Getting ready? For dinner? I mean, I have an empty stomach. I think I'm ready for dinner.

Will laughs.

Will: The girls normally get ready before they go to the final semester dinner. It is the last dinner we will be having.

Ryan: Last?

Will: Oh right, you wouldn't know. After the finals, everyone goes back to their home centres for the holiday.

Ryan: Oh!

A tinge of sadness washes over her. She can't go back to The Bracket. She didn't think she would be welcome there anymore. And even if she did, people wouldn't really act the same towards her.

Will: But some stay here, because of…

Ryan: So, I can stay here?

Will: Yeah. I'm staying here too. I don't really have much going on at my home centre. Seeing you are ready, shall we go in to dinner?

Ryan: Sure!

Ryan and Will enter the cafeteria, an empty cafeteria.

Ryan: Are the boys getting ready too?

Ryan smiles while Will laughs.

Will: Sort of. They have their pacing to do, and a bunch of guys finish up the movie they were watching right before the last final. It's like a sort of tradition.

Ryan: Oh, then shouldn't you go too?

Will: I don't really have to pack as I am staying here, and I've watched the movie they are watching multiple times before. why not spend time with a fellow classmate and maybe friend?

Ryan smiles.

Ryan: That would be nice.

Ryan and Will get their dinner and sit down at one of the many tables. They talk about school, life before coming to Mega Tech. Will couldn't believe the things that Ryan told him about The Bracket. The cafeteria was starting to fill up.

Chapter 6

THE SAND INVASION

A loud bang is heard outside of the building, followed by an almost earthquake-like movement because the floor of the cafeteria seemed to shake. Plates fell off the shelves and shattered on the floor. The loud bang was heard again. The whole building seemed to shake even more, but this time, a part of the wall tore open. The glass of the window shattered as if something had hammered at it. The students started to scream. Most of them cowered to protect themselves from the glass shards. Once it felt safe to run out of the cafeteria, students rushed for the exits. The teachers asked everyone to go a certain way. The white lights that dangled from the ceiling started to flicker and before the students could exit the cafeteria, more of the building's windows shattered. The glass hit a few students. One of them was Ryan. Will grabs Ryan and pulls her out.

Will: Let's go!

Will and Ryan run to the cafeteria door before it closes. There were only five students left in the cafeteria, running to the door. Will takes out his card, swipes it at the cafeteria door and ushers Ryan inside. Ryan hesitates because she would be entering Building 3, but she quicky rushes in as she realizes that she doesn't have any other choice. Ryan waits outside while Will holds the door open for the others. Once the others rushed in and started to run to the exit, Will grabs Ryan's hand and both run towards a dorm room. They reach the door before Ryan realises where they were going. All the lights had gone off. The only light source were the dim overhead lights in the corridor.

Ryan: What are we doing here? We need to get out of here.

Will: We need supplies.

Will swipes his card and runs inside. Ryan follows him because she doesn't know what to do. She sees Will rushing from place to place in his room, getting a bag and stashing things into it.

Ryan: What are you doing? We need to get out of here.

Another loud bang comes from behind them and building shakes again. It felt as if they were about to fall. The screams of students became louder. Ryan turns around and saw students running past the door. She quickly turns to Will.

Ryan: Will, we gotta go. The building is literally about to fall.

Will: It won't. Not at least for the next *(looks at his watch)* seven minutes. Help me get these boxes out of the cabinet.

Ryan looks in the direction Will points. Then she looks towards the door and realises that the screams of students were dying out. The students were leaving the building. She saw tiny boxes, stacked up in the cabinet where Will pointed. She wanted to talk Will out of it, but proceeded to help as fast as she could, because she knew she wouldn't be able to convince him in time. She hurriedly helps Will. Once Will finishes packing, he slings the bag onto his back, grabs Ryan's hand and starts running towards the stairs.

Ryan: Where are we going?

Will: Building 1. Come on, we need to get out of here as fast as possible.

Ryan: Why don't we use the passage that connects the buildings?

Will: It will break any moment now.

At that moment, while Ryan and Will glided down the stairs, she heard a loud crash. She looked out the window and saw the passage split in half. They reached the ground floor and then ran as fast as they could to Building 1. Will led them to the elevator.

Will: Swipe your card!

Ryan: It's going to…

Will: Trust me.

Ryan didn't see any other option. She swiped her card and they both got into the elevator and waited for the doors to close. Ryan saw people running out as the doors were closing. Will pushed a button.

Will: Which floor?

Ryan: 10.

Just as Will pushes the button, they are thrown against the glass. Will being more sturdy stops Ryan from crashing into the glass. Ryan regains her balance and looks outside. They are going up at an abnormally fast speed.

Ryan: Why are we going so fast?

Will: I'll tell you later.

The elevator stops and the doors open.

Will: Let's go to your room.

Ryan leads Will to her room. She frantically swipes her card and the door opens.

Will: Here you go. (*gives her a bag, similar to his*) Grab any clothes that you need and anything that you may need for survival – medicines, anything that you absolutely need.

Ryan opens her cabinet and starts to pack the necessities. She doesn't have much so she finishes pretty fast.

Will: Lets go (*sees the tablet Ryan was holding*).

Will: Leave the tablet.

Ryan: Don't we need i…

Will: Leave it, trust me.

Ryan goes to her desk to keep the tablet and sees a book that her mom and dad had left her. She quickly grabs it. Will takes her hand and they both run to the stairs.

Will: We have two minutes.

Ryan: Two minutes till what?

Will: Till Building 3 collapses and falls onto Building 1. We need to hurry and get out of here.

They both glide down the stairs. Ryan was becoming tired as they went down. The bag's weight wasn't helping either. She felt like stopping. Her heart was pounding in her chest.

Will: Come on! We have just two more floors to go.

The reach downstairs and try to open the door, but it was locked. Ryan frantically looked for her card, but she cannot find it. Will quickly opened Ryan's bag, took out a spare card, swiped it and to their relief, the door opened.

Will: 10 seconds! RUN!!!

Will and Ryan run away from the building as fast as they could. Ryan tries to stop and look, but Will grabs her and tells her that if they didn't keep running the building will fall on them. They kept on running and finally they couldn't anymore. They both looked back and saw the buildings crashing and falling. They then saw something that you only see in the movies or read about in books-a sand creature. There were no other words to describe what Will and Ryan were seeing. It was like a sand tornado, except it had features like legs and hands. But Ryan couldn't make out what it was.

Will: Oh no… no, no, no, no, no!

Ryan: What?

Will: We need to go to school… NOW!

Ryan: School?

Will: We have to! Come on!

Ryan follows Will, but she has no idea where they are going.

Ryan: We won't be able to get there in time. (*looks back and sees the sand-like creature, coming their way, destroying anything that lay in its path*) It is coming this way.

Will looks behind.

Will: Follow me!

They run until they reach a parking area. They see that there is only one bike there. Will and Ryan run up to it. Will, kickstarts the bike.

Will: Get on. We'll get to school faster this way.

Ryan hops onto the bike and clutches the bag Will carried on his back as tightly as she could. Will rode fast, trying to dodge all the cars that had been left on the road. Some of the cars were honking aimlessly. Some looked as if they had crashed. They reach the school.

Will: We need to get to the lab.

They run to the big lab. Will opened a cabinet and took out a box with 'capsules' written on it. He opened it and took out seven round glass capsules out of it. They were about the size of a regular gumball.

Will: Get the other two, we need to get out of here. Put the capsules in the first pocket of the bag.

They rush out of the school building and run away from it.

They then stop because they hear a sound like the gushing of wind coming from a distance. It was getting louder, as if it were coming closer. They looked behind and see a huge whirlwind of sand coming their way.

Will: Ryan, Come here!

Will grabs Ryan and pulls her close to him, he then takes out one of the capsules and throws it on the ground. Before they could turn around, the sand washed over them. Ryan closed her eyes and braced herself, but then she realized that nothing happened to her. She looks around but sees nothing. She extends her arm to make out where she was and she feels a smooth, round surface.

Ryan: Will! Will!

Will: I'm here. Wait! Let me just…

Ryan hears shuffling and then a click. Will pulls out a torch, illuminating the place they were in. Ryan sees that they were in a sort of glass ball. Before she could say anything, she felt a shortness of breath. She was beginning to gasp. Will handed her an oxygen mask and he put one on himself. Ryan put on hers but fainted.

Chapter 7

THE TRUTH

Ryan regained consciousness, and got up. She squinted at what seemed to be a golden lamp, right above her, close to her head. She first thought she was in a hospital, but when her sight became clearer, she realized she was in a gas ball. She sat up and saw Will, sitting across her.

Will: Finally, you're awake.

Ryan: Wha… Where…

Will: You know the capsules we took from the lab? We are in one.

Ryan: We shrank in size?

Will: No, the capsule became bigger to fit us. It was one of the things that the school had come up with. The idea and concept was almost announced. They just had to start creating more copies, before making the idea public.

Ryan: So, let me get this straight. The capsule just got bigger, and now were in it?

Will: Yeah, like a bubble.

Ryan: How are we breathing?

Will: The capsule was designed for situations like this. And because we live in a century of rapid technology advancement, scientists have found ways do many things.

Ryan: How do you know about this? How… how did you know about the building? How…
Will: My parents.
Ryan: Your parents?
Will: Yeah, I am from the centre headquarters of The Sustainers.
Ryan: The centre headquarters?
Will: Yeah, sort of like the capital of all the headquarters of The Sustainers.
Ryan: Oh, ok.
Will: So, when I was on holiday after my first year at Mega Tech, I was at home, doing absolutely nothing, and just thought of going outside. I discovered a door in the central garden that I hadn't noticed before. I opened it and went inside. Actually, I went below. It was some sort of underground place. I went down the steps and heard voices. I heard it all that night. Their meeting went on for hours on end. I heard them planning this very moment.
Ryan: Your parents?
Will: Yeah, and some other people. They were planning to attack the whole planet through Artificial Intelligence.
Ryan: Artificial Intelligence? I thought that was still a theory that was being tested.
Will: Well, this theory was long tested by the centre headquarters and they had started to work on multiple projects. Since then, I never really went back home for the holidays. But because I had planted a very small microchip there, I was able to hear their whole plan. I just didn't know when it was going to happen. AI has gone so far that they are able to bring illusions to life.
Ryan: The sand creature.
Will: Yeah, it was made through AI, and is, as we speak, used

to destroy the whole planet.

Ryan: The whole p-planet? Meaning the…

Will: The Bracket? Most definitely.

Ryan: But why? Why would they do such a thing?

Will: Well…

Ryan: It's inhuman, don't they have some hu…

Ryan stopped in the middle of her sentence, because she realized that his parents were involved too.

Ryan: Sorry, ahh, I didn't mean to say th…

Will: You are not wrong.

Ryan: No, no, let me explain.

Will: Ryan, you are right, they are acting inhuman, and they don't have any sense of humanity. It's because they are not human.

There was a silent pause. Ryan was still processing what Will had just said.

Will: They are not human.

Ryan: What do you mean? What do you mean they aren't human?

Will: After I kept on listening to their conversations, I heard them say, "AI will rule."

Ryan's expression changes, she felt goosebumps on her arm.

Will: I tried to dig for information on my tablet, but all the websites that I had seen said the same thing. AI is a theory, just a theory. Due to its repetitiveness, people tend to believe that AI is…

Ryan: Just a theory.

Will: I had to search even deeper. I managed to find a website with the picture of an article which had my parents and a few others. The articles said that they were the first to go under trial for AI around 10 years ago

Ryan: 10 years ago? I thought you said two years ago.

Will: Well, tests and experiments for AI started around 10 years ago. They called it the Human Simulated Intelligence Project. My parents had been one of the volunteers for that project, and now, they are human stimulated intelligence. When the experiment was successful, the scientists working on it were about to announce it to the world. But unfortunately, the group of people, including my parents, stopped them from doing so.

Ryan: Why?

Will: That's what I was not able to figure out. Anyway, they were able to gain the trust of many high officials in the centre headquarters, and all of them were able to rise up the state hierarchy and become the leaders of The Sustainers.

Ryan: Your parents are the leaders of the Sustainers?

Will: Yeah. They rose up the ranks and about two years ago, started planning to destroy the world. I know this sounds very childish, but destroy the world is what they are doing. They know that if humans were able to make human simulated intelligence, they would be able to come up with something even better and more intelligent.

Ryan: So, they felt threatened?

Will: Yeah.

Ryan: And that is why they want to destroy most of the planet?

Will: Right.

Ryan: But they are only a few volunteers, aren't they? So how will so few people be able to take over the world?

Will: It started with a few volunteers, but now they are a huge group.

Ryan: How do they plan to take over the whole world?
Will: Well, the sand invasion is only the beginning. Who knows what they have planned next.

Ryan couldn't believe this was happening. She thought that The Sustainers had a different mindset, and that she would be able to live the life she had dreamt of, but it felt as if it was all just an illusion.

Will: We will wait a few hours and then got to the surface. This capsule will need an oxygen refill. Want something to eat?
Ryan: I kinda lost my appetite… wait, how would we get food anyway?

Will reaches for his bag and takes out the boxes that Ryan had helped pack. He opened them and revealed tiny balls.

Ryan: Tiny balls, that is our food?
Will: It is modified, so if it's put under heat, it actually becomes food that is edible.
Ryan: What is the physics behind that? How is that even possible?
Will: I have absolutely no idea, but I had taken it from my parents' place and stashed them away in case I ever needed it.
Ryan: Right…

Chapter 8

THE LIGHT ON THE AFTERMATH

Ryan soon fell asleep. It was almost midnight. Will slept soon after. The glass ball was small but spacious and had enough space for them to sit upright and even partially lie down. Both woke up a few hours after because it is hard to sleep when sitting up. They waited until it was 9 pm (according to their watches) to rise up to the surface. Because of the capsule's high technology, the capsule moved up smoothly. Ryan and Will squinted as light entered the capsule. When Ryan opened her eyes, she couldn't believe what she saw-a desert.

Ryan: How on earth are we in the desert?

Will: We aren't in a desert. Well, we are, but we are at the same place we were yesterday.

Ryan: That sand invasion was supposed to make this whole place a desert?

Will: Yeah.

Ryan: So that people couldn't survive?

Will: Yeah…

Ryan: Oh, my goodness! Wait! What happened to the others? Do you think…

Will: Most probably, but when we went to the lab to get the capsules, seven were missing I think there has to be someone around here who must be alive.

Ryan: Wait, then, why did we take 7? Shouldn't have we left them for the others?

Will: There wouldn't be others because as soon as we left, the school building crashed. And plus, we need seven for backup. You never know what might happen.

Ryan: So, if there were seven missing, then they must be somewhere round here, because they couldn't have gone too far. We should try and search for them.

Will: Yeah, it might be hard though. They might be underground.

Ryan: Does each glass capsule have any kind of metal in it?

Will: Most probably.

Ryan: Then I think we will be able to find them.

Ryan goes through her bag and takes out a cube.

Will: What is that?

Ryan: A magnet.

Will: A magnet won't really do much.

Ryan: This magnet will. I designed it. It has immense magnetic pull. Just now, it is enclosed in a material that I tested could lower its magnetic strength. I have an identical one, but what is unique about this that if they are kept in a way to repel each other, they can maintain a constant distance. The only thing is, if we want to find something underground, we have to be moving.

Will: This capsule is a very new innovation.

Ryan: I didn't understand.

Will turns around and places all the bags to the side and moves back. Seeing this, Ryan moves back too. Will then presses the glass. Ryan thought that was not necessary, but the glass lit up as if it were a hologram tablet.

Ryan: Woah!

Will: This capsule has a lot of features, one of which is (*presses a few buttons on the glass)* that from the middle a pedaling apparatus will emerge like the ones in boats where the people have to pedal with their feet to move it. This is how we will navigate ourselves and move.

Ryan: Sweet!

Will presses a few more buttons and a small overhead window opens.

Will: Give me the first magnet.

Ryan gives him the magnet. He slowly pulls off the cover and throws it outside. Ryan then angles the other magnet so that it repels the magnet outside, and the distance between them remains constant. Will then starts to pedal and they begin to move. Whenever the magnet attracted a metal from under the ground, it would sink into the sand. They stopped a few times but were unlucky, because they were just parts of the city buried. They then noticed a pattern; when the object was small, the magnet sank only a little into the sand, but when the object was large the magnet sank further down. So, on the basis of that observation, they searched for two hours but they didn't find anything. They stopped for a break, ate lunch, and then started searching again. Then they found something that was big.

Chapter 9

COMPANY

They went navigated around that area and went in deeper. They turned on their flashlight and a small beeping signal, so that if there was anyone they could get their attention. After looking into complete darkness, it seemed as if there was light on the other side, and the further they went, the brighter it became. Ryan slowed down their speed so they wouldn't bump into anything. They finally stopped. Will increased the volume of the beep so that they could attract the attention of whoever or whatever there was.

Will *(whispers)*: Ryan, be ready for anything. If I say go, back up as fast as you can, stay underneath and pedal fast.

Ryan *(whispers)*: Why?

Will: If it is someone we are not familiar with, they could try to kill us. We need to be alert. I am gonna call out, and if they respond by coming to us and if we recognize them, everything is ok. But if it is not, at my signal, we need to leave.

Ryan: Ok.

Will carefully moves forward, then drags the computer glass setup in front of him, and presses the microphone button.

Will: Hello? Is anyone there? If so, please come closer to the sound.

There is a brief silence, then the lights come closer and closer.

Will: Stay alert and ready.

Ryan nods. After 10 seconds of silence, the light becomes as bright as the one they had on. Will presses another button, letting all the sand between them and whoever or whatever in front of them drain out. Will and Ryan see their two classmates in one capsule. They both let out a huge sigh of relief. Will presses the speech button again.

Will: Let's get to the surface.

Their two classmates nod.

Ryan and Will navigate themselves up to the surface and then see the other capsule slowly emerging from the sand. Ryan moves closer to them and they move slightly closer to Ryan and Will. Will presses another few buttons, and a window opens in the glass capsule. The others do the same.

Will: Matt bro, I knew you had taken a capsule! Hey, Karina!

Karina: Hey!

Matt: Yeah, I had too. *(Looks around them.)* This is crazy, man.

Will: Yeah.

Matt: Have you guys found anyone else?

Will: No, just you guys.

Matt: How did you guys find us?

Will: We went underground after taking in oxygen and then just began to search.

Ryan was about to say something, because Will lied, but she guessed Will had a reason not to tell the truth.

Will: Hey, did you guys find any water?

Ryan wonders why Will asked that. They had water bottles. Maybe for the future?

Matt: No, not yet. We are using bottled water right now. We took one capsule. Who took the others?

Will: Well, there were seven left when we got there.

Matt: Well, I took two. So there must be someone else out there.

Will: They couldn't have gone very far.

Matt: Yeah. I think we should carry on until its around 2 pm and then take a break. We should try and find the others.

Will: Yeah.

Will closes the window and then turns to Ryan.

Will: We will do as we've planned, but we can't trust him much. I'll take over pedaling for now.

Ryan gets off the pedaling seat and sits down against the glass, ready for movement.

Ryan: Why can't we trust them?

Will: I know him, and even though he's my friend, he would do anything to survive.

Ryan: So, you are saying that he isn't loyal?

Will: Yeah.

Ryan: So, are we going to stick with them for a long period or not?

Will: We'll stick with them until the night and leave.

Ryan: How would we do that, without them knowing?

Will: We'll figure it out.

Ryan and Will see the others start to pedal. Will gets ready to pedal, and then follows them. Will types 'capsule manual' into the computer glass keyboard.

Will: Here, read this. You'll know more about this capsule so you get the hang of it.

They take shifts pedaling until its around 2 pm. After a lunch break, they continue to move in one direction, hoping to see some change in the landscape. By nightfall they had seen nothing new. They are still in a desert. They have dinner along with Matt and Katrina.

Matt: Let's go underground for the night and then continue our journey tomorrow.

Will: Sure.

Ryan navigates them underground. Will then turns off their flashlight, and minutes later, the light from the other capsule also turns off.

Ryan: We will stay here for an hour or so and then move.

Will: Why an hour?

Ryan: I know for sure they are not asleep now, and if they are, our movement might wake them up.

Will: Sounds like a plan. I'll leave a note saying we went to look for water.

Ryan: Why leave a note?

Will: We still need them to remain on our side. If we leave, and they find us, we have an excuse-we got lost and couldn't find them. And on the off chance that they are still awake after an hour, they would know why we're leaving, to find water.

Will and Ryan sit around for an hour, waiting for Matt and Karina to hopefully fall asleep. Will leaves a note in the sand, and placed it so that if they moved around, they would be able to see the note. Then, as slowly as possible, they head to the surface.

Will: We would need to leave this area as fast as we can so they can't trail us. Plus, they wouldn't be able to see our trail. The winds are about to start, so the trail will be lost. Would you be able to take the wheel to get out of here fast?

Ryan: Yeah.

They reach the surface, and when they were fully on top of the sand, Ryan pedaled as fast as she could. To Will's surprise, Ryan could pedal really fast.

Will: I am going to turn off the light so that no one can see us. As far as we could see, there is only sand. So, hopefully, we won't crash into something.

Ryan pedaled until they were far enough from where they had stopped before.

Will: I'll take over. We'll go slow, but we need to keep moving, because if they do find out, they could catch up with us.

Will and Ryan set off on their night journey.

Chapter 10

CHOOSING WHERE OUR LOYALTIES LIE

Ryan: Hey, I wanted to ask, why did you stick with me? I am not trying to be rude. Don't get me wrong. I am so thankful that you helped me, or right now, I would probably be dead. But why? I was just curious.

Will: Well, first of all, we had just won our finals together. So, I considered you a friend. You were the only one with me. And if I had not taken you out of there, I would feel guilty. Which is not a good feeling. Secondly, in cases of survival, it is best to be with someone rather than alone because of how humans behave when they are left alone. Also, for some reason, I trusted you. I felt that you weren't the type to betray someone.

Ryan: Oh wow! Thanks!

Will: You are also a very interesting person, who I would very much want to get to know more.

Will smiles at Ryan. Ryan returns the smile. After they had been moving for an hour and a half or so, they stopped, went underground and rested until the morning. The next day.

Ryan: We've been moving aimlessly for almost a day now, we should have found something.

Will: I thought so too, but it looks like they have covered a huge area. But I don't think they have destroyed The Bracket.

Ryan: Why not? Wouldn't The Bracket be one of the first regions they would destroy?
Will: No. If they did, the other Sustainers, who were still loyal to the original pact, would be able to overthrow them.
Ryan: So, they got rid of the threat?
Will: Yeah, but I'm not sure we would be welcome into The Bracket by any chance. By now, they must have got news about the sand invasion. They must be preparing.
Ryan: Not quite. The Bracket had cut ties with any of The Sustainers. So, they have absolutely no idea what is going on in the Sustainer region.
Will: Not even the state?
Ryan: We don't really have a state, more like a president. But that is just a title. Everyone has equal opportunities in The Bracket. It is quite different from The Sustainers.
Will: Ok then, let's try to enter The Bracket and tell them about what is to come.
Ryan: It would be extremely hard.
Will: Right, because they hate The Sustainers.
Ryan: Hate is a strong word.

Ryan smiles. Will too smiles.

Will: You know what I mean.
Ryan: Yeah, but, because I was previously from The Bracket, they might let me in. But chances of that happening are quite low.
Will: It is worth a try.
Ryan: Yeah.
Will: Another problem is how would we get there?
Ryan: Haven't you being reading the manual?
Will: I have, but that doesn't give us a GPS.

Ryan: It does!

Will: Please elucidate.

Ryan then directs Will to the Manual and shows him the first line.

Ryan: See, it says "key features to this glass capsule will reveal itself if you read between the lines."

Will: Yeah, so, isn't it telling us to read the manual to understand the features of the capsule?

Ryan: Well yes, but it also says to read between the lines.

Will: If you are supposed to read between the lines, you would be reading blank spaces. You know that, right?

Ryan: Not quite. If you look closely, there is either a dot or a dash in between each line. It is Morse code!

Will: Morse code?... oh wait, you mean the ancient way of communication?

Ryan: Yeah. Weren't you taught this?

Will: Well, because of tech, we have more advanced ways.

Ryan: There is some truth to that, which means normally people from The Sustainers wouldn't be able to see it. Only people who look close enough would be able to crack it. Don't you see? Whoever wrote the manual and created this capsule predicted something like this, and knew that key features should be displayed to those who would be able to see it.

Will: Ok then, if it is Morse code, what does it say?

Ryan: It gave a pattern of numbers of 0's and 1's and then said 'enter below'. So, I went to the bottom of the manual, tapped around, but nothing came up. Then I tried to tap it in the pattern of the Morse code-small taps for the dots and longer taps for the dashes, and then it revealed a whole secret manual. Wait, let me show you.

Will: Before you do that... How on earth do you know Morse code? Did they teach it to you in The Bracket?

Ryan: No, they didn't teach it to me in The Bracket. My mom and dad's book that they left me had it on the last page, so I just used that.

Will: Oh, makes more sense.

Ryan scrolls down to the bottom of the manual, taps in the code, and then the hidden manual pops up.

Will: Oh my! Wait! You are right!

Ryan: What? So you didn't believe me?

Will: Well, it was hard to. I had started to think you were going crazy.

Ryan smiles.

Will: I am so happy I am wrong. This is a whole new manual. This is great I never thought Kevin would do this.

Ryan: Kevin?

Will: Yeah, Kevin was my older brother, he was the one who designed the capsules and wrote the manual.

Ryan: The one who created the capsules was your older brother? That is so cool!

Will: He told only a handful of people about the capsules, but then he passed away.

Ryan: I am so sorry for your loss.

Will: The sad part is, I have no idea how he died. No one really does.

There was a brief silence. Ryan didn't know what to say.

Will: Well, anyway, at least now I know that his life had a huge impact on others. It seems that you know the hidden manual better than I do, so tell me, how will it help us approach The Bracket?

Ryan: Ok, well, it has a GPS and a tracker of where we are. Let me just scroll down and find a column that says GPS Tracker.
Ryan: Here it is.

She opens the program and a map display comes up.

Will: Wow! This is what we need.
Ryan: Let me find The Bracket.

Chapter 11

GOING BACK

It doesn't take time for her to find it, because, in favor of their luck, they were actually really close to one of The Bracket regions.

Ryan: Wait, we are so close. Oh, my goodness! We can get there in maybe 15 minutes.

Will: I'll ride, you can give me the directions.

Ryan tells Will where to go, and they can see that the sand eventually stops.

Ryan: Stop here.

Will: Why? We can take the capsule all the way there.

Ryan: They won't like it.

Will: Right, but what if we are seen by any of The Sustainers?

Ryan: We could go back in the capsule and escape, but if we want to get into The Bracket and even have a chance of entering, we need to get rid of any technology.

Will: What if they see the capsule?

Ryan: It looks like a glass ball when it has shrunk. They don't have metal detectors. They just search you, and they don't know much about the latest technology, so I don't think they would be suspicious about a glass ball.

Will: That makes sense. Let's go.

Ryan: Because we are on foot, it will take a little longer.

Will and Ryan walk for around 10 minutes, and then The Bracket's border can be seen. Ryan could see the lights in the office turning on. She knew the guards had seen them.

Ryan: Will, listen to me. If they ask about any possession of ours that they may not be familiar with, just say it belongs to our family, and add sentiment to it, they won't ask much about that.

Will: I'll let you do most of the talking.

They approach the guards at the border.

Guard 1: Who are you? And what are you doing here? Sustainers are not allowed here. If you want to meet someonc, you need to issue a request to the president.

Ryan: I am Ryan Sierra. I have lived in The Bracket my whole life until I moved to Mega Tech.

Guard 2: Traitor!

He came closer to Ryan, looking at her with beady eyes.

Guard 1 (to Guard 2): Sierra, you say? Your parents went to War on our side?

Ryan: Yes.

Guard 1: You are allowed in… but not the boy.

Will looks up and then at Ryan, but Ryan doesn't look anywhere. Will looks at Ryan and notices something different about her. She was confident and able to speak for herself.

Ryan: He will come with me.

Guard 2: No, he won't!

Will felt panic starting to build within him.

Ryan: Yes, he will. According to the law book, page 273, section C684, any visitor, former citizen of The Bracket, is allowed to bring one guest into The Bracket. It very clearly doesn't state if that one guest has to be from The Bracket. I am very willing to stay here for you to check the rule book. Even if it means we stay here for long.

Guard 1: She is right, but we will have to check you because…

Ryan: Technology is forbidden in The Bracket. We know.

Guard 2 gives Ryan and Will a disgusted look. Will was surprised at how Ryan had just acted. He had never imagined she could be so strong and confident.

Guard 2: You do not belong here, you traitor!

Guard 1: Calm down or I'll have to report you.

Guard 2 was taken aback. He stared at the other guard as if he had just been betrayed. He then lets out a loud groan and marches back to his cabin and slams the door behind him. The first guard checks Ryan's and Will's bags, their pockets and any belongings they had. He then hands them a pass. The one he gave Ryan stated 'Former B-Ryan Sierra' and the pass that Will got stated 'Sus S-Guest-Ryan Sierra.'

Guard 1: According to the rules, you are allowed into The Bracket for only 24 hours, and if you are not here by the end of 24 hours, we will send a few guards to escort you ourselves.

Ryan: Thank you!

The guard then proceeds to open the gate.

Ryan: Just one more question. What is the name of the community we are about to enter?

Guard one: The Carreens.

Chapter 12

HOME, NOT WELCOME

Ryan and Will went through the gates and into the community. Ryan's heart had flipped when the guard said that they were at the Carreens. She was home. She never thought she would ever be able to come back and meet Blaire and Ms Jane.

Will: So, we don't have a map. Where do we go? Do we just keep walking until we see someone?

Ryan: I am home.

Will: What?

Ryan looks at Will, her eyes start to tear up but she does not cry.

Ryan: Will, I am home.

Will: This is where you used to live?

Ryan: Yeah, The Carreens. This was my community.

Will: So, the people here would welcome you, right?

Ryan: I am not sure about that, but I know just the person to go to right now.

Ryan's heart starts to beat faster and the buildings become more familiar. She leads Will into The Carreens. She knew exactly where all the people would be right now-the hall-for the usual community lunch. Ryan had to go to Ms Jane's house, because she knew Ms Jane would be the only person who would welcome her. She couldn't go to Blaire's house because her parents didn't have as open minds as Blaire and Ms Jane. The only problem was Ms Jane's house was right next to the hall. She had to find a way to meet her without the others knowing.

Ryan: Let's go this way.

Ryan leads Will through a narrow alleyway.

Will: Why are we going this way?

Ryan: The person's house we need to meet is right next to the hall, where everyone is having lunch. I don't want to gather much attention. I know a way I can get Ms Jane's attention without the others knowing, but for that, we need to go to her backyard.

Ryan and Will reach Ms Jane's backyard. It was beautiful. There were roses, daisies and many other flowers. There was a pathway leading to the backdoor, outlined with pebbles.

Will: She sure has a beautiful backyard.

Ryan: Yeah, she always has. We need to hide.

Will: Will those bushes do?

Will points towards a few bushes next to a tree, about 10 m away from the roses.

Ryan: Perfect, you go there., I'll try to get her attention.

Will quickly hides behind the bush. He tries to keep Ryan in his sight. He sees Ryan pick up a few rocks from the pathway, and place it in the middle, he then hears laughter and noise of conversation from the behind the house. He saw Ryan jerk her head up and then run towards the bushes. Ryan came up to Will and hid with him.

Ryan: If Ms Jane still remembers, she will know that we are here.

Will: We?

Ryan: Well, me. But she wouldn't mind if you are there.

Will: She wouldn't?

Ryan: Let us just say that she is more open-minded than any of the people in The Bracket.

Ryan and Will wait for 10 minutes. Then they notice the door handle turning. Ms Jane walks out with a bucket. The second she sees the stones, she almost drops the bucket and looks around.

Ryan: Come on!

Ryan gets up, Will follows. Ms Jane sees Ryan and Will. Ryan waves to Ms Jane. Ms Jane waves back. She goes back into her house, and then comes out and urges them to hurry and come inside. Ryan and Will run towards the house, while Ms Jane keeps a lookout. Once Ryan and Will are inside, Ms Jane locks the backdoor, rushes to the front door and locks it too. She draws all the curtains and then goes towards Ryan and Will.

Ms Jane: Ryan!

Ryan does not say anything. She runs into Ms Jane's arms and hugs her.

Ms Jane: Ryan! What are you doing here?! And who is-

Ryan looks at Will and urges him to come closer.

Ryan: This is Will… a friend I made at Mega Tech.

Ms Jane: Hi, Will! Nice to meet you.

Ryan: I came here to tell you something very important.

Ryan and Will tell her everything that had happened to them, and what they think is going to happen now.

Ms Jane: I knew it.

Ryan: You did?

Ms Jane: Well, not exactly that, but I had a feeling something like this would happen.

Ryan: But The Sustainers are not bad people.

Ms Jane: Oh dear, I know that. Of course, The Sustainers are

not bad people. But ever since HSI started, I knew it was likely to happen. I predicted it would happen in the next year.

Will: Wait, how did you know about HSI? I thought The Bracket citizens didn't know or cared about The Sustainers in any way.

Ryan: Her husband.

Will: What?

Ms Jane smiles at Ryan.

Ryan: Your husband is in The Sustainers?

Ms Jane: Yes, yes, he was.

Ryan: How on earth did I not figure it out before?

Ms Jane: You couldn't have. My husband and I separated during World War III. He was in The Sustainers and I was here, in The Bracket. I wanted to go to The Sustainers, but it was too late, too much damage had been done. But we always managed to meet once a month at the border. It has been working for years. We communicated through the telephone and no one knew about us-just the guard at the border.

Ryan: Was he the one who let us in?

Ms Jane: I am quite sure. He knew a lot about you and your parents. Once you mentioned your name, he probably didn't ask you much.

Ryan: yeah…

Ms Jane: That kind of communication was working perfectly, until the month, when he came to visit and he told me about the HSI and how he was a volunteer for it. I had a terrible gut feeling about it, but I didn't say anything. A month after that, he came as an HSI. Some things had definitely changed, but he was still the same person I knew… until about two years ago. He started to change a lot. From his behavior to his attitude. I just thought it may have been because of stress, but the month I saw him after the changes, I did not recognize him. He looked exactly like my husband but he was not. He had changed completely. I remember that conversation very vividly. It was not like the other conversations we had. It was different, and he didn't remember one thing that we always did every month-it was then that I knew he was not my husband anymore. Since then, our calls went from a call every day to a call in a week to a call in two weeks, then to him not coming the next month, and eventually, all communication was cut off. Remember Ryan, when you first called me from Mega Tech, and I abruptly left, it was because it was the day of the month that my husband used to meet. Since two years ago, I haven't talked to him. But for the first time in two years, I had got a message to go to the gate. That is why I left so abruptly. The guard at the border gave me a letter that my husband wrote to me two years ago.

Ryan: Why couldn't he give it to you then?

Ms Jane: He knew that whatever was in that letter couldn't have been handled by me back then.

Ms Jane goes to a shelf and pulls out a letter.

Ms Jane: This was the letter that he gave me.

Dear Jane,

I don't know if I would be able to give this to you, but I wanted to tell you something very important. Remember when I volunteered to take part in the HSI project? Well, as I told you, it went successfully, but recently, there have been more and more HSI's. I thought the scientists were getting ready for the launch of the results, and wanted to test it out on more, but I just overheard the other HSI's and the scientists have no clue about the increasing number of HSI's. It has been a project that the HSI's were working on their own. When I asked them about it, they said there was going to be an official meeting about it. Something is telling me that whatever happens at the meeting will not be good. I think something is about to happen. If I change and something about me is off in your opinion, the next time I meet you, please know that something big might happen. I don't know when, where and how, but I know for sure that something big will happen.

Love,
Terry

Ms Jane: Nothing big has happened, but now that you have told me this, it might as well be soon enough.

Someone knocks on the door. The three of them exchange panicked looks.

Ms Jane: Hide!

Will and Ryan go into another room, and hide in the closet. They hear the door open and close. They hear two sets of voices.

Ms Jane: Ryan, Will, it is all ok.

Will and Ryan slowly come out of the closet, but don't go out of the room yet.

Will: What if Ms Jane is compromised?

Ryan: That's what I'm thinking too.

Ms Jane *(from the other room)*: Ryan, its Blaire.

Ryan's heart beats faster. She hasn't seen Blaire in a long time. She rushes out of the room and looks at Blaire standing in the doorway. She was carrying her blue purse that she always carried around. Blaire gives Ryan a hug.

Blaire: Oh my goodness, Ryan, you are here!

Ryan: Yeah… yeah, I am here! How are you?
Blaire: I'm ok. What are you doing here? And who is that? *(points at Will, who was slowly and reluctantly coming out from the room)*
Ryan: A friend.

Ryan and Will re-tell their story to Blaire.

Ryan: We do not have much time.
Blaire: What do you think is going to happen?
Will: We don't really know.
Ryan: All that we know is that whatever is going to happen, it is going to happen soon.
Ms Jane: It will most likely happen in the next 12 hours.

Ryan, Will and Blaire all turn their heads towards Ms Jane.

Will: What do you mean?
Ryan: Next 12 hours?
Blaire: How?
Ms Jane: The sand invasion that occurred at The Sustainers happened around a day or so ago right?

Will and Ryan nodded.

Ms Jane: If the HSI are as intelligent as we think, they would plan to attack sooner than later, because eventually, The Bracket will most definitely find out one way or another, and that would not be good for the HSI. So, to remove all the threats immediately, they would get rid of The Bracket in the next 12 hours.
Ryan: Ok, if we go with that theory, then we need to alert the others, right?
Blaire: We can't.
Ryan: Why?
Blaire: No one would believe us.

Ms Jane: We do not have a choice. we need to tell the others; it is the least we could do.
Will: Even if we do tell them and on the off chance that they believe us, what will we do?
Ryan: Try and move away from the communities.
Will: Even so, if the HSI want to get rid of us – theoretically, destroy the world-they would desertify it-so if there were any living beings, they would have a low chance of surviving on earth.
Ryan: He's got a point, and they did desertify not only The Sustainers' regions, but also the space in the middle of it.
Blaire: What if we go underground?
Ms Jane: That won't work because there will be very limited oxygen, and if we try to escape, the sand might fall, and we won't be able to survive.
Ryan: Then what do we do?
Ms Jane: I have an idea, but we would have to work fast.

Chapter 13

THE WAREHOUSE

Ms Jane managed to disguise Will and Ryan, and then, along with Blaire, set off on foot to get to her destination.

Blaire: Where are we going?

Ms Jane: Some place where we aren't allowed to go.

They approached a place with cycles.

Ms Jane: Get on one, we will reach there faster.

Will: I'm not that good at cycling-I'm not that fast.

Blaire: I could stay behind with Will and Ryan and Ms Jane, you could take the lead.

Ms Jane: Are you sure?

Blaire: Positive.

Ms Jane: Then let's go.

They all get on the cycles and Ms Jane takes the lead.

Will: Thank you for staying behind with me Blaire.

Blaire: No problem!

Ms Jane and Blaire cycle faster and Will and Blaire who are behind them, slowly catch up. Soon they reach a warehouse. It looked extremely old and rusty. Parts of the roof were broken, and the nearer they approached, the stinkier it got.

Ryan: What are we doing here?

Ms Jane: You'll see.

Ms Jane and Ryan park their cycles, and close behind arrive Blaire and Will. They all go into the warehouse, which smelled of dead rats.

Will: Goodness, the smell! What are we doing here?

Ms Jane remained quiet. Ryan and Will exchanged confused looks.

Ms Jane: Blaire, remember in P E you guys had strength training?

Blaire: Yeah.

Ms Jane: Well, let's test it out, shall we? Come here, help me get this heavy box off this table.

Blaire goes to help Ms Jane. A small hint of jealousy hit Ryan, because she felt a little detached from Ms Jane and Blaire. Normally, if Ms Jane required help, she would ask both of them. Ms Jane and Blaire manage to get the heavy box off the table.

Ms Jane *(Looking at Will and Ryan)*: Come here, you two!

Will and Ryan join the others around the table. Ms Jane bends down and looks underneath the table. Blaire, Will and Ryan exchange confused looks. They hear a sort of button click. Silence. Ms Jane stood up.

Ryan: What…

The table lit up. The whole warehouse became illuminated with the light emitted by the table. The four of them squinted at the bright light. Blaire, Will and Ryan were amazed.

Blaire: What? What is this?

Ms Jane: This is the technology that we used before World War III.

Ryan: How is it still here? Does The Bracket allow it?

Ms Jane: Each community in The Bracket has this warehouse, and only around four people from each community know about this.

Will: But why?

Ms Jane: Will, trust was lost, when World War III broke out. Even though there was an official agreement between the people of The Bracket and The Sustainers, the former was not able to trust the latter because they could start another war using technology. And The Bracket did not want to use technology. The president elected four people from each community to preserve the little technology we still had from before the war. Now, I would like to give you more information about this, but we are running out of time. This table acts like a tablet. Ryan and Will, I am sure you know about this.

Ryan and Will *(in unison)*: Yes.

Ms Jane: Well...

She presses a button that was in the centre of that table tablet, and suddenly the rotten shelves and wood in the warehouse start to retreat into the walls.

Blaire: How is this... what?

Ryan looks at Blaire and smiles because she finally gets a chance to experience the wonders of technology with her best friend. Looking at the amazement on Blaire's face as the room completely changes into a sort of tech lab reminds Ryan of her first day at Mega Tech.

Blaire: Woah! Is this how your school was?

Will: It is different in some ways, but more or less, yeah, this is how the room functioned at Mega Tech.

Ms Jane: Ryan and Will, I am sure you would be able to navigate around this place, and understand how it works. While you do that, I will contact the rest of the communities.

Will: Sure thing.

Ms Jane: Try and tell Blaire about it too, so that she becomes familiar with the technology. It would be helpful.

Ryan: Ok.

Ms Jane contacts the other communities while Ryan and Will look around and see what they could use for their survival. Ryan tells Blaire everything she knew. Blaire, on the other hand, was finding it hard to even comprehend.

Blaire: Wait... wait, Ryan, what is the Internet? I have heard you say that word a number of times, but I do not know what it means.

Ryan: Ok so, the Internet is…

Ryan explained to Blaire about the Internet, and all the other things that she had learned at Mega Tech. Blaire was fascinated.

Blaire: Oh, Wow! That is amazing! I wish I had gone to Mega Tech.

Ms Jane: All right, I have contacted the other communities. They are on it, and they will also try and convince the others. Our mission is now to use the resources here to find out a way to survive. What do we do?

Silence from everyone.

Will: Ok, ok, ummm… Ryan, we can do this. We did so during the quiz, and we have done this kind of problem solving in class too. Come on, we can think of something.

Ryan: That was just class! This is real life.

Will: Why did we do this in class? To use it if we ever needed to in real life, and right now, we do. So, come on, let's work together as a team and we will be able to figure it out.

Ryan: Ok… so where do we start?

Ms Jane and Blaire watch Ryan and Will try to solve the

problem.

Blaire: They seem like they know what they are talking about.

Ms Jane: Yeah, they do.

Ms Jane looks at Ryan and smiles. She knew that Ryan would flourish into a very smart and caring human being, and she was glad that she as there to witness it.

Ms Jane: In the meantime, let us try and think of a way we could convince our community.

All four of them work on their jobs. Blaire and Ms Jane thought of ways to persuade and convince their community. Will and Ryan were not getting anywhere near a possible solution for their survival.

Will: Ah! That won't work.

Ryan: Let's start again.

Will: We have been doing exactly that! We have looked at every possible resource here.

Ryan: Not all of them. Remember the bunch of glass outside the warehouse?

Will: Yeah, what about it?

Ryan: Well, Ms Jane said that everything in this warehouse had something to do with technology. So maybe those huge glass pieces have some technological value.

Will: Ms Jane?

Ms Jane: Yes?

Will: Did you see those huge glass pieces outside the warehouse?

Ms Jane: Yeah, what are we going to do with that?

Will: We just wanted to know if they had any technological value?

Ms Jane: Yes, they do! Oh my! Why didn't I think of that?

Will: Could you please elaborate?

Ms Jane: Those glass pieces are actually meant for windows, but not just as windows, they have many technological features… one of the features I remember is that one could code it to become strong – However, there is a limit though I am not quite sure. You could add features like how much they can expand and, I am not sure if it could happen, but it can also provide temporary oxygen.

This sounded familiar to Ryan and Will. They looked at each other.

Both *(in unison)***:** The glass bubble!

Ms Jane and Blaire exchange confused looks.

Blaire: Glass bubble?

Will to Ryan: I'll get the glass from my bag.

Ryan to Will: Ok.

Ryan: Have you guys found a way to persuade the others?

Blaire: A few ways, yeah.

Ryan: Great! Ok, so, you can go and try and persuade the community, Will and I will work on a way to survive.

Ms Jane: Ok…

The table tablet pings. Ms Jane goes up to it.

Ms Jane: It is a message from the other communities. They want to know how to survive. What do we tell them?

Ryan: Once we have figured it out, we will message them the instructions.

Ms Jane types out the message.

Ryan: I'll message them from the tablet. You two should go and try to convince the others. We don't have much time.

Ms Jane and Blaire head back to the community, while Will and Ryan figure out a way using the glass pieces.

Ryan: Will…

Will takes out the glass ball from his backpack and looks at Ryan.

Will: Yeah?

Ryan: Would it be ok to use your brother's designs to make this? I mean, it was your brother's invention.

Will: Of course, it is ok! And I know what you are going to say next. That we would be telling others about this. I know we are but my brother made these glass balls to help people survive, and if we don't tell the others, it would defeat Kevin's purpose in making this.

Ryan smiles.

Ryan: Ok then!

Chapter 14

BUILDING SHELTER

Ryan and Will tell the other communities of their plan. They were able to connect the computers to the glass pieces outside, and then they started to code and manufacture something similar to the glass ball. They tried to explain everything to the other communities, but because the people hadn't used technology in years, they were very slow to understand it all. Finally, Ryan and Will finished coding the glass pieces, and then sent the code to the other communities so that they could use it to. By the time Will and Ryan had finished coding, Ms Jane and Blaire came back to the warehouse along with some people.

Ms Jane: We are here.

Ryan: Great!

Ryan looks at the people who had come. There were not that many. Will notices the same thing.

Will: Where are the others?

Blaire: They refused to come.

Ryan: What do you mean?

Ms Jane: They didn't believe us.

Ryan: There has to be a way.

Blaire: We tried everything.

Ms Jane: Well, we cannot do anything about it. Let us just start building the safe house now, as we have company to help us.

Will: Ok, so here is the plan.

Will explains everything that is to be done to construct the safe house, and due to his knowledge, the people were even more convinced and agreed to help. This was a very good sign, but Ryan knew that there were others she could convince if she had gone back to the community.

Ryan: Ms Jane?

Ms Jane: Yes?

Ryan: I am pretty sure there are some other people who would come, I know it.

Ms Jane: We tried, Ryan. Blaire and I tried our best, but the others wouldn't budge.

Ryan: What if Blaire and I go? I could try.

Ms Jane: I am not sure it would make any difference, but go ahead, and come back as quickly as you can.

Ryan: Ok, Blaire, let's go. We are going to try and convince the others.

Blaire: They wouldn't budge earlier.

Ryan: Let's try again. I am not giving up.

Blaire: Ok, I'll get the cycles ready.

Ryan: I'll just tell Will.

Ryan approaches Will while Blaire goes out to get the cycles ready.

Ryan: Will, Blaire and I are going back to the community.

Will: Why?

Ryan: I think we could convince some of the others.

Will: Do you think it will work?

Ryan: I am not sure; But I would feel guilty if I didn't try.

Will: Well, I can't really say no, can I?

Ryan smiles.

Will: Ok, go, but take this.

Will reaches into his pocket and takes out one of the seven glass balls they took.

Ryan: Why?

Will: If anything happens, then at least you and Blaire will be safe.

Ryan smiles.

Ryan: Thanks!

As Ryan walks away, Will grabs her hand.

Will: Please be safe, you cannot die.

Ryan: I won't, trust me.

Chapter 15

GAINING TRUST

Ryan and Blaire approach each house and ask them to meet at the common hall area.

Ryan: At least some people turned up.

Blaire: I am sure more people will turn up. They will not want to miss this.

Ryan: I guess.

Blaire: You can start, and I'll pitch in.

Ryan: Ok, here we go.

Ryan looks at the people who showed up. She almost went off because of the disgusting looks that the people were giving her.

Ryan: Hello, everyone, good evening!

Person in the crowd: Betrayer!

Ryan: I am here, with Blaire to convince you all to join us for your own safety.

Another person from the crowd: TRAITOR!

Ryan: Ok listen up, I did not come here to be called a betrayer or a traitor, I actually would not have come if I didn't care about all of you. Yes, I went to Mega Tech. Are we all not given a choice? If you didn't want me to go to Mega Tech, why would you give us the choice of going to Mega Tech? Anyway, I have come here to plainly warn you guys.

Person from the crowd: Warn us about what? Something that The Sustainers are cooking up to overthrow The Bracket? Bull shi…

The head of the Carreens from the back: Enough! What is going on here? Blaire, why are you on the platform? And Ryan, who gave you permission to be here?

Ryan: Ms Mayor, I understand your concern but I have a very valid reason and I would like to voice my concerns and try and help this community.

Mayor: Why would you do such a thing? Aren't you now a Sustainer, our enemy?

Ryan: With all due respect, although I had moved to The Sustainers, I still cared about The Bracket as it has taught me things I would have never learnt in The Sustainers. And I respect all the attributes that The Bracket aspired to, because they have made me who I am today. But, unfortunately, The Sustainers are demolished.

The crowd gasps and bursts into conversation.

Blaire whispers to Ryan: Why are we telling them this?

Ryan: You guys didn't tell them?

Blaire: No, because we thought the people would become very joyous, and some powerful people here would try and take advantage of the situation.

Ryan: Valid point, but anyone here wouldn't stand the chance of overthrowing, no offense, but you don't know the extent to which the intelligence of the HSI extends to, they are extremely powerful-literally more intelligent that the human species.

Mayor: QUIET! Ryan, would you care to explain the accusation you have made?

Ryan: Reverently, this is not an accusation, it is the truth. If you give me permission, I would like to tell all of you what happened to a friend of mine a day ago, and also what is going to happen.

Mayor: We are listening.

Person form the crowd: No, we are not. She is a traitor, why should we listen to her?

Blaire: She is not a trai…

Mayor: Stop!

The Mayor shuffles to the front of the crowd. Both Blaire and Ryan start to worry because they thought the mayor would say something to them, but instead, the mayor turned to the crowd.

Mayor: Yes, Ryan had gone over to The Sustainers, but that doesn't mean we forget our manners and our code of how we behave in a group setting. So please, remain quiet and listen to the two girls. Make up your own mind after you have heard them. Girls, go ahead, and be quick.

Ryan: Thank you, the day before yesterday was the Mega Tech's finals day. All the students gave their last exam and headed back to their dorms to celebrate. Unfortunately, this celebration could not have happened because a huge Sand Invasion took place, where people engineered sand so that they demolished the school buildings, and all the infrastructure that The Sustainers had built. A friend of mine and I survived because no one knew about us as far as my friend and I know. Most of The Sustainers are dead because of the sand invasion. My friend overheard a meeting being held, and he can confirm that there is a new species emerging called the HIS or Human Stimulated Intelligence. The HSI's plan was to demolish the human species so that they would be able to essentially rule the world. And they can. The only way they can do that is by decertifying the world. They already did the Sustainers, now, their mission is The Bracket. We want to save you all, and this is why we are asking you to come with us and help build a survival shelter.

Blaire: Please do believe us, we do not want anything but your safety. Both Ryan and I have been with you all since we were babies, and we have grown up with you guys. You should know that we don't mean any harm. We will always protect our roots. And besides, we can do only so much to convince you all.

Silence. Blaire and Ryan look at each other, worried that people would start to criticize them.

Mayor: How can you be so sure that they will attack The Bracket?

Blaire: They got rid of The Sustainers first because they know that if they attacked The Bracket first, The Sustainers would find a way to overthrow the HSI's. That is why they first demolished The Sustainers, and then they plan to demolish The Bracket. They know that the people of The Bracket do not use technology. Regardless of that fact, most of The Bracket citizens had lived a life before World War III. Hence the people would still know a bit about technology. The Bracket became a threat, and that is why their next target, is us.

Silence. The Mayor looks at Ryan and Blaire.

Mayor: Well, as you said, you can only do so much to convince us.

Blaire and Ryan's hearts dropped, because they thought they had been able to convince the Mayor. But they had not, obviously. Tears filled Blaire's eyes because she had lost hope, but Ryan didn't.

Mayor: I believe you.

Blaire and Ryan look up at the Mayor in shock. As much as they wanted to hear those words, they were still surprised.

Mayor: Not completely because the story does seem bizarre, but this situation is possible.

The Mayor turns to the rest of the crowd.

Mayor: I do believe these girls, but I cannot force you guys to join them, so, it is your choice. Girls, the people who do want to go with you, what would they need?

Ryan: A bicycle and a small bag with clothes and any necessary belongings. Please do not bring bags, because we have very little space.

Ryan and Blaire got off the platform and approached the Mayor.

Blaire: We are glad that you believe us.

Ryan: We got to convince at least one person to go.

Looking at the crowd, who was most certainly listening to their conversation, she was hoping that someone would speak up and say they would want to join them too, but no one, everyone just either kept staring at them, or away from them.

Mayor: Blaire, you have been a true member of The Carreens, and hence I believed you, and know that you have good intentions. As for you, Ryan Sierra, you left us, but it is true what you said, you grew up with us, and that has made you who you are. And if our community taught you any good, then I trust that you also have good intentions.

Person 1 *(from the crowd):* I'll go and my family.

Everyone looks at the person who just spoke. It was a tall man, dressed in an ironed, red-checked shirt, surrounded with someone who seemed to be his wife and two children. A few others spoke up as well. Ryan and Blaire exchanged happy looks.

Blaire: Anyone who wants to join us, please be ready in 10 minutes. We will meet at the Glass Bowl post. Bring your cycles, because it will be the only way we could get there in time.

Ryan (*to the Mayor*): Thank you so much for believing in us. You have no idea how much we appreciate it.

Chapter 16

SURVIVAL

Ryan and Blaire cycle up to the Glass Bowl Post on the outskirts of the community. Slowly people started to show up. Ryan and Blaire were glad that they were able to convince people. On their way to the Glass Bowl, Blaire was able to convince the families of some of her classmates as well, and they too started to show up. When 10 minutes had gone by, and there were no other people in sight. Blaire and Ryan led the 20 people to the warehouse. Both of them noticed that the stinky smell of the warehouse had gone away. They also noticed that the glass pieces were finally starting to come together. Ms Jane comes out of the Warehouse and is amazed by the number of people she saw. She went up to Ryan and Blaire.

Ms Jane: Oh my! You guys took so long. I cannot believe this. How did you guys manage to convince so many people?

Mayor: With a very convincing story!

Ms Jane and the Mayor start to chat, while Blaire and Ryan go into the warehouse to help Will.

Ryan: How is it going?

Will: Oh, you guys are back! Thank goodness! Ok, so when we were checking each glass piece before assembling it, we found that we coded a part of each glass. Apparently the glass pieces can extend, which is a good thing, but we need to code them as well in order for the circuit to go all the way. And for it to function, I was able to code 25 percent of the glass, but it is taking a lot of time. I already told the other communities.

Ryan: Can't we just copy and paste the code? I mean it is the same after all.

Will: I tried doing that, but it didn't work. And instead of wasting time trying to see why it wasn't working, I just started to code all of them manually.

Ryan: Ok, that is good thinking. That would take time, however. I'll help with the coding.

Blaire: I'll help the others assemble the glass pieces.

Ryan: Ok. And also, ask Ms Jane to explain to the others what is happening, so no one is left in the dark.

Blaire goes out to help the others.

Ryan: Almost all the glass pieces are outside, and to maintain the oxygen level, we need to manufacture the glass for those. So, let's first do that so they are able to provide oxygen to all of us.

Ryan and Will start to code the glass pieces so that they are manufactured for survival, and the others start to build the shelter. Unfortunately, just then there was lightning and thunder. Ryan and Will rush outside to see what was going on.

Will: What the heck?

Ryan: I thought they were going to desertify us.

Ms Jane: What is going on? I thought it was going to be a sand invasion.

Will: Maybe this is not their doing. Maybe it is just the weather

Lightning struck again, and this time the time the thunder followed soon after.

Ryan: You are probably right.

The winds start to become stronger.

Ryan: Regardless, we still need shelter. We don't know what will happen. There are a bunch of coats in one of the cabinets. You could give it to the others, so that even if it rains, people will be able to work. We need to build this shelter as quickly as possible.

Ms Jane hurried outside to alert the others, and people came inside to get the coats. Will and Ryan continue to code.

Will: Done!

Blaire comes into the warehouse.

Blaire: We are almost done!

Ryan: I just need to add… done! I added more strength to it for the rain.

Will: How? I thought I was able to find its limit?

Ryan: I would explain right now, but we need to help the others.

Blaire: Grab a coat. It is pouring outside.

Ryan and Will grab a coat and rush outside to help the others. Ryan couldn't get a thought out of her head-she saw people who were not sure and that they did want to go, but they didn't out of fear. Ryan ran to her cycle. She knew she still had time to get a few others.

Will: RYAN!

He had to scream because the winds were stronger and the rain started to fall even more heavily.

Will: RYAN! WHAT ARE YOU DOING?

Ryan: I need to get the others.

Will: NO, DON'T GO! IT IS TOO DANGEROUS.

Ryan: I HAVE TO GO! I'LL COME BACK SOON. I PROMISE.

Ryan cycled away before Will could say anything.

Blaire: Where is Ryan?

Will: She is gone!

Blaire: Where?

Will: To get the others.

Blaire: IS SHE OUT OF HER MIND?

Ryan fights the wind and rain cycling as fast as she could towards the community. She could barely see, but she didn't stop. She went to the houses of the people she knew she would be able to convince and then helped them gather their things and told them where to go. Directions to the warehouse weren't that hard to convey. And she did that under five minutes with two families. She went to a few more houses, but they didn't budge. So, she heads back to the warehouse. The two families she convinced would have reached there by now. On her way, she looked back towards the community, and saw something she did not want to see-the sand invasion. It was covering the land very fast. She sped towards the warehouse, but her legs were becoming tired. Thankfully, she remembered that she still had the glass ball with her, so she quicky got off her cycle and activated the glass ball. She did it just in time. The sand covered the glass ball the second she went into it. She waited a minute, and then started to navigate herself back to the warehouse. She wasn't able to access the map because the rain interfered with the signal. Fortunately, she managed to reach the warehouse.

Blaire (*inside the warehouse)*: Where is Ryan?

Will: Didn't she make it? Didn't she come with the others?

Blaire: No… oh no, no, no, no, she can be… RYAN? RYAN!!!

Blaire shouts her name, but Ryan is nowhere to be seen in the shelter. Will goes around the crowded shelter, trying to find

Ryan, but she wasn't there.

Blaire: Will, do you think…

Will: No, I know she is alive. She has to be.

Will approaches the corner adjacent to the door because he knew that if Ryan used the glass ball, she would bump into the warehouse on the corner. He waited 10 minutes before he heard a thud. He grabbed his computer to push away the sand from that part of the shelter glass, and saw Ryan, in the glass ball, wearing an oxygen mask. Somehow, Ms Jane, Blaire and Will manage to get Ryan into the Shelter.

Will: I told you! You shouldn't have gone. Oh my goodness, Ryan!

Blaire put a towel around Ryan.

Blaire: What the heck, Ryan?

Ryan: There were two families I convinced. Were they able to come? Did they make it?

Will: Yes, they made it.

Ryan: Thank goodness!

Will: Never do that again!

Ryan: Let's hope there won't be a next time.

Will smiles and hugs Ryan.

Chapter 17

TWO YEARS LATER

Two years had passed since the Sand Invasion. A lot of things have happened since then. The HSIs discovered the communities, survivors, all over the region. Instead of demolishing them, or forcing them to become HSIs, they let them be. They thought it would be nice to see some people inferior to them. The Sustainers who survived had either been lucky or had joined the communities. But the majority of The Sustainers who had survived were made HSIs. All the HSI's lived in the capital, Chicasca. Chicasca was essentially the world's capital. There were about 30,000 people left on earth. Around 20,000 were HSI's and 10,000 humans, living in communities. The HSIs had become another species. In the last two years, they had reproduced and produced offspring who were more intelligent than human children. The HSI's sent food to the communities, but it was very little, so the communities had to introduce rationing. The communities, although scattered all around, came closer to each other. There would often be meetings between the communities, but otherwise, nothing much happened. Or so the HSIs at Chicasca thought. The communities had made an organization called The Sustainers, although the name is a little ironic seeing that the majority of the communities consisted of ex-citizens of The Bracket. They gave that name to the organization because they wanted to bring back the earth that was earlier and sustain the good that existed before. Being former citizens of The Bracket, they weren't that fast with the little technology they had, but were able to learn quickly because they were born before World War III, and knew how technology functioned before the war.

Present Day

The operation was called Project S, and its two leading agents were Ryan and Will. They were to go to Chicasca and try and bring them down. Both of them were 18 now and had grown close. Blaire and Ms Jane were the other two agents. They would be navigating and helping Will and Ryan from their organization headquarters (which was one of the community shelters). Will and Ryan were able to install a chip in their head and then add sheets of make-up so that it looked like skin. They did this because in order to help them move across the Chicasca border. An electronic monitor at the border checked that whoever went into Chicasca had Stimulated Intelligence installed in the head because that is how HSIs are stimulated to become more intelligent, a mere chip inserted in their brain. Ryan and Will didn't know if it would work, but they gave it a try. They head towards Chicasca. They approach the border and because the HSIs knew that no human would be able to pass the electronic monitor, they kept the borders open. Will held Ryan's hand.

Will: Let's go.

Ryan nodded. They both closed their eyes, and stepped across the border. They waited for something to happen, but nothing. They were successful.

Ryan: It worked!

Will: Yeah, I'll send a ping to Blaire to tell them that we made it.

Some guards approach them.

HSI Guard 1: You guys can take a break, there are orders from the Captain that now the guards will only be at their posts for 10 slots throughout the day. Here are your key cards for the new location to the guard stay. Your other card won't work even if you want to communicate, so you can hand them over.

Will and Ryan look at each other.

Will: We will keep those cards as a souvenir.

HSI Guard 2: Whatever. Oh, and also, now it is mandatory that each guard wear the mask given. The masks will be in your rooms.

Will and Ryan nod, while keeping their heads down. The guards walk away.

Will: That was a safe call.

Ryan: Damn, we could have been caught, if they didn't think we were guards. Ok so, we need to get to the guards' quarters. Thankfully, we now have masks, and we would probably know the schedule of the guards who we are supposed to be, so we would be able to get more into the city.

Will: If we are supposed to be two guards, then the HSIs that we are supposed to be monitoring the communities. We need to quickly go to the guard quarters and alert Blaire and Ms Jane so that they can ask the others to take care of them.

Ryan: But what if they try to communicate with the other guards?

Will: All the guards have new cards, and they said that the old cards won't work now, so, they wouldn't be able to communicate.

Ryan: Right, so the only thing is to ensure that those two not be able to make it to the Chicasca border.

Ryan and Will go to the guards' quarters, go to their rooms, find a schedule and their masks. They continue their supposed guard duties so that the HSIs won't suspect them. They need to figure out a way into the main quarters of Chicasca to know how to shut down the chips in the HSIs' brains. After a week of staying there, they start to make their move. Because of their guard privileges, they get into the main quarters of Chicasca. Will is taken aback when they go up the elevator. He saw his mom and dad on a billboard on one of the buildings.

Will: Ryan!

Ryan: Yeah?

Will: Look!

Points to the billboard.

Will: My parents.

Ryan: Oh my goodness! They are the head of Chicasca.

The elevator doors open, and they get out and go somewhere there weren't any people.

Will: I cannot believe this.

Ryan: Neither can I.

Will: How Ryan? How could my parents do this?

Ryan: I don't know, Will.

Will: They only volunteered.

Ryan: Who knew all of this would happen?

Will: Ahhh…

Ryan: Quiet! Someone might hear us. Listen, I understand that it is devastating that your parents are the head of Chicasca, but I still have to do something. Listen Will, if you don't want to be a part of this, it is ok, I understand. It is hard to face that, but I need to go. And, those people you saw on the billboard, they are not your parents.

Will looks at Ryan. She could see that Will was tearing up, even under the mask. Ryan took his hand.

Ryan: They are not the same people who volunteered to be part of the HSI programme. They are changed beings. They are not your parents. They…

Will: You're right. They changed ever since they volunteered, and they stopped being my parents. Come on, let's go.

Ryan reaches out and gives Will a hug.

Ryan: Ok, we would need to take the stairs, because it would be rarely used, assuming that people in this building only use the elevators.

Will: Good idea.

Ryan and Will take the stairs to the top floor from where everything is controlled. They open the door and enter a room with glass walls. There was a lighting table tablet in the middle of the room with hovering programs. They also saw someone on a chair, facing the window.

Man in the chair: Hello, long time no see, Son?

Will's eyes widen. It was his dad.

Will: Hello, Jim!

Ryan's eyes widen as she realized what is happening. She moves closer to Will.

Jim: Ah Will, since when do you call the old guy by his name?

Will: You are not my father.

The chair turned around to reveal Will's dad.

Jim: Ah, yes! We stopped being a family a long time ago.

That sentence smote Will's heart. Even though he does not consider Jim his father anymore, he expected a little sadness from Jim but then he recalled that Jim was a HSI and that they have less emotion.

Jim: I am sure you and your girlfriend over there are trying to shut us down.

Ryan and Will are shocked.

Will: How…

Jim: We have known ever since you got here.

Will: Then why didn't you do anything?

Jim: I wanted you here and face you. How do you think you were able to get into this building without me letting you? Huh? You thought you were smart? Ha!

Will's anger exploded. He banged the table tablet. Ryan stopped him from doing anything else.

Ryan: Will!

Jim: Oh Ryan, let him, he is still a small boy, isn't he?

Silence.

Jim: Ok now, shall we proceed?

Ryan: Proceed with what?

Jim: With your elimination, and then the rest of the communities.

Will: NO!

Jim: Oh yes. Now, who first. You? (*Points at Ryan)* or you (*Points at Will)*.

Will: You don't have any weapons here.

Jim: How can you be so sure?

Ryan: We scanned this room. This is the only room in the whole of Chicasca whose glass windows are made of just glass because the technical glass would have interfered with your control centre.

Jim: Smart! You should have joined us. But you are wrong.

You see, the perks of being an HSI is that you still have human features.

Will: You are going to fight us?

Jim: I will eliminate you.

Jim ran towards Ryan and starts to fight her. Ryan fights back but he is too strong. Will jumps in and stops Jim from killing Ryan. Ryan was able to escape Jim's hands. Will punched Jim in the face as hard as he could.

Jim: You will regret this.

Jim and Will continue to fight. Ryan took this chance to run over to the table tablet and tried to shut down the HSI. An alarm starts to ring all over the city. Ryan and Will have to shut down the HSI programme before other people come in. The software asked for a password. Ryan starts to panic. She didn't know the password. She types in 'human stimulated intelligence' but it didn't work. She had only one attempt left.

Ryan: Will! It needs a password.

Will: Try the full form of…

Ryan: I already tried that, it didn't work.

Jim was struggling in Will's arms.

Jim: Ha-ha!

Ryan tried to think. Then she remembered something from the book that her parents gave her. She opened it and looked for the words. She typed in 'newerahsi' and it unlocked. There were three buttons labelled male HSI and female HSI. She looked up at Will, and saw he was getting choked by Jim. She quickly pressed the male HSI. As soon as she clicked the button, Jim fell to the floor.

Will: You did it!

Ryan: Only the male.

Will's mother barges in.

Jill *(Will's mother)***:** STOP! do not press that button.

Ryan: Why not?

Jill: We can offer you anything – just name it – but do not press that button.

Will: She is lying.

Jill turns to Will.

Jill: Oh, my son! Will! I am not lying. We will help you, we will live in harmony.

Will: I really wish that was true.

Will grabs Jill's hand.

Will: Mom, I really wish you weren't lying.

Will's voice breaks. Ryan could tell he was sad about all this, about his parents.

Will: Ryan, press the button.

Jill: NO!

Will: Now, Ryan, press the button.

Ryan presses the button, and Jill falls to the floor. The lights of Chicasca start to close. Only the building they were in was illuminated in the city.

Chapter 18

THE CESSATION, THE CONCLUSION

The buttons that Ryan pressed sent a huge electromagnetic shockwave throughout the region and messed with the chips in the HSIs and knocked them out. One would assume that the HSIs without their chip would become humans again but it was a little more complicated than that because the chips were inserted into their brain. Their brains were severely damaged as a result and they perished. The electromagnetic wave even affected people in the community who were not in the shelters. The people in the shelter were secure due to the technical glass. Ms Jane was one of the people affected. She fell into a coma, but according to the few doctors who remained, she was getting better. Ryan and Will got back safely to the community. Ever since then, the environment started to heal itself. The community let the environment be for a while.

3 months later

Will and Ryan are trying to develop a system that is able to detect misuse of technology in a certain region automatically, in order to view changes and possibly prevent any further invasions. It is a far reach, but both of them are determined to help the planet grow sustainably and safely. They both had already participated in various regeneration programs, helped around to bring back life to earth. Chicasca was no longer there. Ryan thought of recycling the materials from Chicasca to help grow society in a more sustainable manner.

Will: Ryan, got the system ready to go?

Ryan: No (she says as she curls her mouth into a frown)

Will: We'll get it soon, don't worry, doesn't hurt to try again.

Ryan: we've been working on this for so long now.

Will: And we have made progress! We'll get there, just gotta keep trying. For now though, lets take the evening off.

Ryan: We don't have to go back to base until 8pm.

Will: who said we would go back to base?

Will and Ryan take the evening off and climb the tallest hill in their area, and lie under the stars.

Ryan: I still can't comprehend all the things that have happened.

Will: Me either, it all seems like a dream.

Ryan: Yeah.

Will: I am glad that I've met you during this whole…experience

Ryan: I'm happy to have met you too.

Both smile at each other. They lay under the stars and appreciate the universe they are in.

What major harm could 10,000 people possibly cause? Earth was regaining its natural beauty. Will, Ryan and the people left on the planet, all worked together to continue building a better place. It was a new beginning for all of them. A chance to right their wrongs. Start a new life without HSI, a life, with Real Intelligence.

OR WAS IT?